The 'Civilisational Mission'

The Imperial Archives

FROM DISCOVERY TO THE CIVILISATIONAL MISSION: ENGLISH WRITINGS ON INDIA

Volume 5

The 'Civilisational Mission'

Editor

Pramod K. Nayar

B L O O M S B U R Y

NEW DELHI • LONDON • OXFORD • NEW YORK • SYDNEY

BLOOMSBURY INDIA
Bloomsbury Publishing India Pvt. Ltd
Second Floor, LSC Building No. 4, DDA Complex, Pocket C – 6 & 7,
Vasant Kunj, New Delhi, 110070

BLOOMSBURY, BLOOMSBURY ACADEMIC INDIA and the Diana logo are trademarks of Bloomsbury Publishing Plc

First published in India 2022
This edition published 2022

Bloomsbury Academic
An imprint of Bloomsbury Publishing Plc

ISBN: HB: 978-93-54356-00-1; ePDF: 978-93-54358-39-5
2 4 6 8 10 9 7 5 3 1

Printed & bound in India by Replika Press Pvt. Ltd.

CONTENTS

PREFATORY NOTE

The archival texts have been retained in their original font, style and content in order to clearly show the environment of the time when these documents were produced. It is important to show in a book such as this the views held at that time and the profound effect they had on society. We acknowledge that several of the texts are derogatory about Indians, women and communities of different religious faiths like many hundreds of other colonial-era-based works. While these are clearly unacceptable to us today, we have not attempted to change any wording or redact the texts so that the contemporary reader may experience the rhetoric, attitude and ideologies that so clearly marked the Raj. In places, where the text had been smudged and rendered impossible to read, that specific segment has been deleted.

We would like to make clear that these are not the views held by the editor or Bloomsbury India and do not reflect our mission and values which are clearly stated on our website (https://www.bloomsbury.com/in/connect/about-us/missions-and-values/)

GENERAL INTRODUCTION: ARCHIVE AND EMPIRE

That the British writings on India occupy over several miles of shelf space in the British Library, London, is an apocryphal tale, but one which *may* have substance, given that there was no aspect of the subcontinent that did not pique the curiosity of the British or generate some document or the other.

In his *The Imperial Archive: Knowledge and the Fantasy of Empire* (1993), Thomas Richards demonstrated how the documentation (the subject of considerable work, notably in Bernard Cohn and others) and archivisation not only produced knowledge about the colonies but were also instrumental in generating the fantasy of absolute control. And yet, it is never easy to read these records produced by a diverse set of English, Irish and Scottish missionaries, administrators, men of leisure, nurses, teachers, wives and/or sisters of the men who occupied official posts in the colony, soldiers, mercenaries and others—many of whom, for many reasons, had their own dynamics and tensions with the *English*.

Several approaches to the imperial record exist, and this introductory chapter sets out some of them.[1] In the process, it also flags what the archive does in terms of the imperial structure and processes.[2]

The Power of the Archive

The archive is not a mere compilation of what John Malcolm (1823) advised his officers on the right approach to the native officers, or what Thomas Williamson (1808) described as the potential for the hunt in India. The archive is not a passive reflection of imperial power—it constitutes and constructs it. As diverse commentators—such as Cohn's work on the 'survey modality' (1997) and C.A. Bayly's *Empire and Information* (1999)—have pointed out, the Empire ran on information,

[1] I use the term 'imperial archive' throughout to refer to the corpus of published material across genres, as diverse as maps, geographical accounts, census reports, travelogues, administrative reports, ecclesiastical documents.

[2] These volumes work only with the print archive of British India, although a vast archive of visual material also exists, and has been the subject of significant studies. See, for example, Guégan (2011), Chaudhury (2012), Pinney (2014), Dohman (2017) on colonial photography, and Tobin (1999), De Silva (2011), Eaton (2013), among others, on colonial/imperial art and paintings.

and information-gathering constituted not just an act of power but was a *constituent* of the power structure. It classified, organised and legislated on the subject peoples, through the census, the geographies and anthropological studies. In the process, it defined who is counted as a subject/citizen. For instance, writing about the Todas or the Gonds, and then examining the numbers of Muslim students in schools, both the educationist and the statesman were constructing model imperial citizens who would benefit, resist or accept from 'modern' education. In other words, the imperial archive on education was not merely advocating 'modern' education: it was constructing *educate-able* citizens from among their colonial subjects while abandoning the others. Thus, archivisation and informatisation were ultimately about the power wielded over the identity-making and rights of the subjects.[3]

Relatedly, the archive and the documentation also made the subjects *visible to themselves*. With 'modern' education, for instance, the Indian colonial subject in school or college came to identify themselves in particular ways. They learnt what it means to be a good citizen, to be modern, to develop and demand certain skills, etc. They recognised their location on the civilisational scale in the books they read and assimilated (*primitive* and *non-modern* as opposed to the modern European). In an argument that resonates with my claims above, Antoinette Burton and Isabel Hofmeyr write about the power of the English book:

> The embodiment of English manly authority, the book was not simply 'a surrogate Englishman in his highest and most perfect state,' it was the very emblem of imperial sovereignty—with the rigorous spine a testimony to its singularity, its probity, its titular power ... books impressed themselves in the everyday lives of imperial subjects, manifesting the formal values of an elite or bourgeois self and modeling in their material form the coherence and commanding presence of British imperial power itself. (2014: 1–2)

The colonial subjects were told, through these English books, what kind of spiritual and moral training was required for them to 'improve'.

---

[3] It must be noted that it was not only the human subjects in the colony that became objects and subjects of the imperial archive. Fauna and flora, climate, landscape and topography—indeed the natural world in its entirety—were also archived. For studies, see Edney (1997) and Damodaran et al. (2015), among others.

As A.H. Benton of the Indian Civil Service wrote in *Indian Moral Instruction and Caste Problems*:

> [The Indian] People are on the whole kindly, docile, alert, keen-spirited, high and low, one of the best-mannered peoples in the world, and they would appear to offer a very promising field for right spiritual treatment. (1917: 92)

The education archive, and especially its insistence on moral training and moral apprenticeship of the subjects as a *preliminary* to training for political citizenship, was built on the

> founding assumption … that the native readership of English texts, and the recipients of English education, were amenable to their teachings, which led them to abandon their traditional manners and disciplines. This necessitated a solid moral training to make them good citizens. (Nayar 2020: 142)

The archive also, frequently, captures the rift and fracture within the colonial subject's responses to, say, Western/English education. See, for instance, Syed Mahmood's anguish about the Indian Muslim's refusal to accept this education:

> Such feelings of aversion towards English education entertained by the Mahomedans … stand in sharp contrast to the attitude of the Hindu community…. This difference in the sentiments of the two communities towards English education, is the real key to the reasons of the vast disparity of progress of English education which the two nationalities have respectively made. The effects of this disparity have been most baneful to the interests of British India in general, and to the Mahomedan community in particular. (1895: 23)

In time, the colonial subject, convinced of the 'truth' in the power of the Englishman's word or photographic record, not only accepted the arguments about their inferiority but also welcomed the interventions in the form of the civilisational mission of the Empire. The archive had, therefore, produced the *willing* colonial subject.

In particular cases, such as Thuggee, the archive enabled the colonial structures of law enforcement and the judiciary to enact legislation and, in the process, demonise specific cultural practices. Examining the Thuggee archive, Alexander Macfie writes:

> [W]hereas Sleeman and his colleagues tended to define the activities of the thugs in terms of wickedness, murder, deceit, cowardice and criminality, the thugs themselves tended to evaluate them in terms of courage, enterprise, bravery, daring, cunning, adventure and martial

> skill … in terms usually associated by both the British and the Indians with the heroic values of war. (2008: 396)

The Archive, the Coloniser, the Colonised and Cultural Exchanges

Shifting focus, Antoinette Burton has demonstrated how the imperial archive also fed into the coloniser's psyche, imagination and political imagination. A pithy summary of how the imperial corpus fuelled, inspired and controlled the social imaginary, policies, attitudes and responses of the Britons in the nineteenth century is available in Burton's *Empire in Question*. Victorian culture, writes Burton,

> as a racialized landscape shaped by decades, if not centuries, of colonial peoples, goods, and ideas coursing through its highways and byways … as always already imperial not just implicitly but as part of a pedagogical meta-narrative about the relationship of modernity to the world-historical phenomenon of colonialism in world history…. (2011: 2–3)

Burton proposes that English 'sensibility' was shaped by Britain's imperial role and character, and its concomitant racialised hierarchies—thus makes the production and consumption of texts (and commodities) about and from the colonised peripheries central to the making of Britain itself (also see Hall 2002).

The archive also instantiates, other than the racialised power binaries (white/black, coloniser/colonised), cross-cultural *influences* and *exchanges*. Contacts across races, ethnic groups and the coloniser–colonised divide were frequent through the colonial period.

The English language took into itself words from their colonial subjects. They also sought to document the grammars of the languages of the subcontinent for their own officers and staff. As a consequence, a vibrant field of cultural exchanges opened up in the languages, with Indian pandits and English philologists and grammarians collaborating. The imperial archive in this domain shows mutual influences of English on Indian languages and vice versa (including Sanskrit [Naregal 2001]) but also the *organisation* of knowledge around the latter (Lelyveld 1993; Rao 2004; Mir 2010; Auer 2014).[4] Scholars—the famous 'Orientalists'—translated texts from, say, Sanskrit into English. Organisations and societies, such as the Asiatic Society, the

[4] A detailed annotated bibliography on these and other aspects of English colonial discourse on India can be found in Nayar 2021.

Zoological Survey of India, the Archaeological Survey of India, were spaces through which the English statesman, *memsahib* and trader encountered Indian temples, art, food practices, superstitions, systems of healing, among others.

English literary texts, as numerous commentators have shown (Leask 1993; Teltscher 1997), began to introduce Indian 'themes' and motifs, whether the *sati* or the wealth of the country's landscape. This field of literary studies was one of contestation and adaptation (Vishwanathan 1990). Be that as it may, the circulation of the English novel in nineteenth-century India catered to the Indian audience attuned to the melodramatic and informed their own creative work (Joshi 2003). Other commentators like Harish Trivedi (1993) have noted how English literature was received in India and the transactional nature of this reception.

Local experts, *writers* and translators were an integral component of the East India Company and the British government. Even account and trade books were produced through a collaborative project (Ogborn 2007). In other domains, such as translations, Indian scholars like Kasinatha Bhattacharya enabled the work of Charles Wilkins (Davis 2015).

Manners, protocols of civic interaction and norms of social, interracial interaction were also sites where cultural exchange and mutual influence were visible. Even the idea of 'civility', as Anindyo Roy has argued, was treated by the native—and projected as such by *English* textbooks and teachers—as markers of 'modern progress and mobility' (Roy 2005: 11). Therefore, both English and Indian commentators (Webb 1915; El Edroos 1922) produced advice and courtesy books for Indians and Englishmen in India (Nayar 2016, 'Civil Modernity'). These contained suggestions like:

> Members of each class, without entering into political or official discussions and avoiding personal remarks, may have much pleasant intercourse by asking about and describing the manners and customs peculiar to each other's nationality, or about their art, music, poetry and literature.... Talk about sport is most suitable at club. (El Edroos: 89)

The Archive and the Global

Another approach to the imperial archive chooses to see the archive as instantiating not just the sensibilities, attitudes and modes of the British coloniser and the subcontinent's colonised, but as enabling *global and globalising imperial networks*. That is, the archive is seen as embodying not just the binary of an imperial 'centre' and 'periphery' (the colony), but a vast network of global connections. We see this interpretation in the work of John Darwin.

In *The Empire Project: The Rise and Fall of the British World-System, 1830–1970* (2009), Darwin shows how the 'interdependence' of various regions and colonies shaped the British Empire in four specific domains. First, there is the military interdependence of various geopolitical regions:

> the most obvious forms of such inter-dependence were naval and military.... British ability to provide naval protection or to send reinforcements to the scene of a conflict would have been very limited without the resources the imperial system supplied. It was strategic control of the Cape Colony (whose economic value was derisory before 1870) that secured the naval gateway to Asia from European waters. The prime function of Egypt, occupied by the British in 1882, was to preserve British use of the Suez Canal and protect the 'Clapham Junction' of imperial communications. Malta, Aden, Ceylon, Singapore, Hong Kong, Esquimalt (on Vancouver Island), the Falklands and Halifax, Nova Scotia, formed the network of bases from which the Royal Navy patrolled the world's sea-lanes. India played several roles in the British world-system, but perhaps its critical function was to be the main base from which British interests in Asia could be advanced and defended. Indian soldiers and a British garrison paid for by Indian revenues were the 'strategic reserve' of the British system in Asia. Because India played this role, other British possessions and spheres east and south of Suez were largely exempted from the costs of defence—a fact of crucial importance to their economic viability. (3–4)

Then there is the commercial interdependence and linkages:

> Both colonial territories and 'informal' colonies had to compete for investment and credits from London to expand their economies ... with the grand exception of the United States (which had received one-fifth of British foreign investment by 1913), British capital was shuttled by the City of London between the various sectors of its commercial empire (a vast global realm among whose key provinces were Canada, Argentina, India, Australia, Southern Africa, China and the Middle East), employing a calculus of prospective return and speculative gain. (4)

The third domain of such connections would be the demographic interdependence:

> Although two-thirds of British migrants went to the United States up until 1900, almost all the rest were distributed between the four main settlement zones of Canada, Australia, New Zealand and South Africa. Indeed, their economic development was usually seen as being closely dependent upon drawing labour and skills from the British supply.... Between 1834 and 1937, India exported some 30 million people to other British possessions as indentured labour, and perhaps one-fifth remained as permanent settlers. In the tropical empire (which British migrants avoided) they supplied much of the labour and business expertise to promote commercial expansion. (4–5)

Finally,

> the spheres of British expansion were progressively linked by a complex system of communication. From the 1840s onwards, this was provided by subsidised mail services, telegraph wires, undersea cables, an expanding rail network, fast passenger steamers and (in the twentieth century) imperial air routes. (5)

In consonance with the work of Darwin, other commentators have mapped these global connections and interdependencies of the British Empire. Thus, Tony Ballantyne, Jonathan Hyslop, among others, in their contributions to the *New Imperial Histories Reader*, map racial imaginings and knowledge formations, working-class presences across the Empire, from India to Australia and Southern Africa. The migration of people and goods in the 1850–1914 period, argue Gary Magee and Andrew Thompson in *Empire and Globalisation: Networks of People, Goods and Capital in the British World, c. 1850–1914* (2010), was instrumental in the making of an international economy. This, of course, put tremendous pressure on the colonised peoples but also made '"transnationalism"—living in and identifying with more than one country or place—a normal way of life for many British people in the half-century before 1914' (5); an argument that resonates with that of Antoinette Burton about Victorian England cited earlier.

Alan Lester's work in the field of imperial humanitarianism and the 'civilisational mission' has made similar connections to argue for a trans-imperial history. Through the late eighteenth and the nineteenth centuries, notes Alan Lester, we can discern the rise of a 'moral geography of the globe', where the Europeans felt responsible for 'distant strangers' (2000: 278). Thus, imperialism intersected with, fed into and drew from humanitarian ideologies and thought in *different* parts of the world/Empire. Subsequently, Lester et al.'s work focused on not 'national boundaries' (Britain's) but on 'transnational and trans-imperial connections' (2020: 2). They argue that 'the principles of freedom, civilisation and liberalism that motivated them were dissolved in a solution of violent racism through which British power was applied' in *various* colonies and geographical locations (2). Through a reading of three years—1838, 1857 and 1879—and the archive of Victorian imperialist statesmen and legal luminaries like James Stephen, Lester et al. demonstrate the linkage and common foundations (ideological, racism, etc.):

> [T]he ending of slavery and the rise of free trade doctrine, repeated Indian famines and the Uprising of 1857, the First and Second Afghan Wars, the First and Second Opium Wars, the Great Xhosa Cattle Killing and the Anglo-Zulu War, mass emigration from the British Isles, the self-governance of settler colonies in North America, Australasia and southern Africa and the devastation of Indigenous societies. (11)[5]

The Archive in 'New Imperial Histories'

The modes through which the archive has been read and employed have come in for criticism in the *new imperial history* turn. Nicholas Dirks summarises the problem with the slide between the production of the imperial archive and the production of the historical events within imperialism. Dirks writes:

> Begins the histories behind and beneath the production of the kinds of primary sources that have represented colonial knowledge even as they have been used to determine and justify colonial policy. The archive has enshrined, in [Michel] Foucault's sense, this raw material

[5] Philippa Levine and John Marriott in their Introduction to the massive *The Ashgate Research Companion to Modern Imperial Histories* (2012) argue that for many commentators, such as C.A. Bayly, 'modernity' in Europe itself is a consequence of its imperial actions—'The putative simultaneity of Europe's imperial ascent, globalisation and the birth of the modern world has led many to see an intimate interconnectedness.' (2)

However the trouble with this reading is, they note, 'that not only did Europe (or the west if we include the Americas) continue to display significant characteristics that might be regarded as pre-modern, but many of the features identified as modern were to be found equally in societies beyond and often unconnected to Europe.' (2)

> for subsequent historical representation. In the Indian case, the archive is both the precipitate of the history of conquest and rule and the basis on which that history has been written by colonial administrators. (2010: 95)

This 'colonial history' most notably in the 'Cambridge School' of historians, argues Dirks reading the archive of John Seeley and others, was in fact 'colonial fiction', which forwarded the idea that 'Indian politics emerged as a direct reflex of administrative initiatives set in motion by colonial rule' (95). Dirks continues:

> [such colonial histories argued] that local elites, the very groups that had been the collaborators for British rule, turned nationalist—in the context of participation in the progressively enlarged electoral arenas of provincial and municipal politics—when they realized that more of the pie could be obtained through autonomous political institutions than through colonial ones.... (95)

This meant

> [The Cambridge School] proved its arguments by using colonial sources—frequently police records and confidential files—that documented the spurious activities of nationalist figures in what was a large-scale colonial effort to track, contain, and debunk the very politics that sought to overthrow colonial rule. (96)

More recent readings have shown how colonial and imperial legacies and their discursive remains, even in the postcolonial era, turn to and retain its ideologies and representational modes. Nadine Attewell writes in *Better Britons*:

> [in] the afterlife of empire insofar as the projects of nation building with which it is concerned ... sexual reproduction [is the] key to, and a potent figure for, the (re)constitution of the national body after the 'end' of empire. (2014: 6)

This implies that the archive and the historical record—even as we debate what counts as the historical record—is very much an active constituent of the present postcolonial thought and actions as well.

*

The volumes here are only a small sample of the imperial archive. The range and depth of the archive are impossible to encapsulate in a few volumes. While I have made attempts elsewhere to capture some of this variety (Nayar 2007; 2009; 2013; 2016 [*Siege and Prison Writings*]; 2017; 2019), much more is required and possible. For example, the visual archive of the Empire, with its modalities and aesthetic grammars of 'composing' the subcontinent, whether in photography or painting (some of which may be found in Archer 1972), requires much more presence in the form of collections.

The present volumes focus on select aspects of the imperial archive: the accounts of 'discovery' and exploration—flora and fauna, geography, climate—the people of the subcontinent, English domesticity and social life in the subcontinent, the wars and skirmishes—including the *Mutiny* of 1857–1858—and the *civilisational mission.* It excludes legal documents and the many Acts and laws enacted by the British government.

Volume I consists of documents that deal with England's *discovery* of India, its exploration and mapping of the Indian land. This volume includes material as diverse as the letter from India of Thomas Stephens, often called 'the first Englishman in India', chorographic and cartographic accounts from geographical, meteorological, archaeological surveys that the various organisations and societies established for the purpose produced.

Volume II includes English studies of Indian languages and the social order. Ethnographic surveys of the subcontinent's people and cultural practices were published from the late eighteenth century. Practices like female infanticide, sati and thugee, seen as emblematic of the 'barbarous' Oriental, received special attention in the documentation. The characteristics of various tribes and ethnic group were also mapped in considerable detail.

Volume III shifts the focus entirely to the English home and social life. The documents include advice on gardening—an integral part of the English home—and on housekeeping. In the latter, the English were given instructions on how to monitor the domestic economy and manage the servants. Advice manuals on hunting and field sports were also published. Given the interracial dynamics at work, officers were issued manuals on etiquette and behaviour. Accounts of hill-stations and camps, and the social life in the Presidencies make up the rest of the volume.

Volume IV is a collection of accounts of a very different British life in India: as prisoners, under siege and in conditions of war. Starting with the notorious *Black Hole* of Calcutta to the 1857 *Mutiny*, the English wrote about being assailed, besieged and tormented in their war journals and prison accounts. These documented physical and emotional suffering, the losses of families and lives, even as they strove to depict British grit and determination.

Volume V documents England's *civilisational mission*. These documents offer a glimpse into British opinions and strategies on diverse subjects. It includes Macaulay's (in)famous Minute of 1835, accounts of medical missionary activities, views on establishing missionary activities and the British views on women's education.

Works Cited

Archer, Mildred. *Company Drawings in the India Office Library*. London: HMSO, 1972.

Attewell, Nadine. *Better Britons: Reproduction, National Identity, and the Afterlife of Empire*. Toronto: University of Toronto Press, 2014.

Auer, Blain. 'Early Modern Persian, Urdu, and English Historiography and the Imagination of Islamic India under British Rule', *Études de Lettres* 2–3 (2014): 199–206.

Bayly, C.A. *Empire and Information: Intelligence-Gathering and Social Communication in India*. Cambridge: Cambridge University Press, 1999.

Benton, A.H. *Indian Moral Instruction and Caste Problems: Solutions*. London: Longmans, Green and Co., 1917.

Burton, Antoinette and Isabel Hofmeyr. 'Introduction. The Spine of Empire? Books and the Making of an Imperial Commons'. In *Ten Books that Shaped the British Empire: Creating an Imperial Commons*, edited by Antoinette Burton and Isabel Hofmeyr. Durham and London: Duke University Press, 2014.

Burton, Antoinette. *Empire in Question: Reading, Writing, and Teaching British Imperialism*. Durham and London: Duke University Press, 2011.

Chaudhury, Zahid R. *Afterimage of Empire: Photography in Nineteenth-Century India*. Minneapolis: University of Minnesota Press, 2012.

Cohn, Bernard S. *Colonialism and Its Forms of Knowledge: The British in India*. New Delhi: Oxford University Press, 1997.

Damodaran, Vinita, Anna Winterbottom and Alan Lester, eds. *The East India Company and the Natural World*. London: Palgrave Macmillan, 2015.

Darwin, John. *The Empire Project: The Rise and Fall of the British World-System, 1830–1970*. Cambridge: Cambridge University Press, 2009.

Davis, Richard. 'Wilkins, Kasinatha, Hastings, and the First English *Bhagavad Gītā*', *International Journal of Hindu Studies* 19, no. 1–2 (2015): 39–57.

De Silva, Prasannajit. 'Representing Home Life Abroad: British Domestic Life in Early Nineteenth-Century India', *Visual Culture in Britain* 12, no. 3 (2011): 313–331.

Dirks, Nicholas B. 'Coda: The Burden of the Past.' In *The New Imperial Histories Reader*, edited by Stephen Howe, 92–105. Oxford: Routledge, 2010.

Dohman, Renata, ed. *Empire and Art: British India*. Manchester, UK: Manchester University Press, 2017.

Eaton, Natasha. *Colour, Art and Empire: Visual Culture and the Nomadism of Representation*. London: I.B. Tauris, 2013.

Edney, Matthew. *Mapping an Empire: The Geographical Construction of British India, 1753–1843*. Chicago: University of Chicago Press, 1997.

El Edroos, Aboobaker. *Modern Indian Etiquette: Of Mixed Society, Describing Ancient Social Usages and Important Indian Manners and Customs, Aiming at Social Amity Between Indians and Non-Indians*. Surat: H.R. Scott at the Mission Press, 1922.

Guégan, Xavier. 'Visualizing Alienation: Symbolism and Duality in Samuel Bourne's Photographs of British India', *Visual Culture in Britain* 12 no. 3 (2011): 349–365.

Hall, Catherine. *Civilising Subjects: Colony and Metropole in the English Imagination, 1830–1867*. Chicago: University of Chicago Press, 2002.

Joshi, Priya. *In Another Country: Colonialism, Culture, and the English Novel in India*. Oxford: Oxford University Press, 2003.

Leask, Nigel. *British Romantic Writers and the East: Anxieties of Empire*. Cambridge: Cambridge University Press, 1993.

Lelyveld, David. 'The Fate of Hindustani: Colonial Knowledge and the Project of a National Language'. In *Orientalism and the Postcolonial Predicament: Perspectives on South Asia*, edited by Carol Breckenridge and Peter van der Veer, 189–214. Philadelphia: University of Pennsylvania Press, 1993.

Lester, Alan, Kate Boehme and Peter Mitchell. *Ruling the World: Freedom, Civilisation and Liberalism in the Nineteenth-Century British Empire*. Cambridge: Cambridge University Press, 2021.

Lester, Alan. 'Obtaining the "due observance of justice": The geographies of colonial humanitarianism', *Environment and Planning D Society and Space* 20, no. 3 (2000): 277–293.

Levine, Philippa and John Marriott, eds. *The Ashgate Research Companion to Modern Imperial Histories*. London: Ashgate, 2016.

Macfie, Alexander Lyon. 'Thuggee: An Orientalist Construction?' *Rethinking History* 12, no. 3 (2008): 383–397.

Magee, Gary and Andrew Thompson. *Empire and Globalisation: Networks of People, Goods and Capital in the British World, c. 1850–1914*. Cambridge: Cambridge University Press, 2010.

Mahmood, Syed. *History of English Education in India, Its Rise, Development, Progress, Present Condition and Prospects. Being a Narrative of the Various Phases of Educational Policy and Measures Adopted under the British Rule from Its Beginning to the Present Period (1781 to 1893)*. Aligarh: M.A-O. College, 1895.

Malcolm, John. 'Notes of Instructions to Assistants and Officers Acting under the Orders of Major-General Sir John Malcolm, GCB.' In *A Memoir of*

Central India: Including Malwa, and Adjoining Provinces, Vol. 2, edited by John Malcolm. London: Kingsbury, Parbury and Allen, 1823.

Mir, Farina. *The Social Space of Language: Vernacular Culture in British Colonial Punjab*. Berkeley: University of California Press, 2010.

Naregal, Veena. *Language Politics, Elites, and the Public Sphere: Western India under Colonialism*. New Delhi: Permanent Black, 2001.

Nayar, Pramod K. 'English Discourse and India'. *Oxford Bibliographies Online*. New York: Oxford University Press, 2021, https://www.oxfordbibliographies.com/view/document/obo-9780190221911/obo-9780190221911-0114.xml.

______. 'Civil Modernity: The Management of Manners and Polite Imperial Relations in India, 1880–1930', *South Asia: Journal of South Asian Studies* 39, no. 4 (2016): 740–757.

______. 'Moral Readership and Political Apprenticeship: Commentaries on English Education in India, 1875–1930'. In *The Edinburgh History of Reading. Vol. IV. Subversive Readers*, edited by Jonathan Rose, 138–161. UK: Edinburgh University Press, 2020.

______. *Colonial Education and India*, 5 vols. London: Routledge, 2019.

______. *Days of the Raj: Life and Leisure in British India*. New Delhi: Penguin, 2009.

______. *English Siege and Prison Writings: From the 'Black Hole' to the 'Mutiny'*. London: Routledge, 2016.

______. *Indian Travel Writing, 1830–1947*. 1830–1947, 5 vols.

______. *The Penguin 1857 Reader*. New Delhi: Penguin, 2007.

______. *Women in Colonial India: Historical Documents and Sources*, 5 vols. London: Routledge, 2013.

Ogborn, Miles. *Indian Ink: Script and Print in the Making of the English East India Company*. Chicago and London: Chicago University Press, 2007.

Orsini, Francesca. *The Hindi Public Sphere: Language and Literature in the Age of Nationalism*. Oxford: Oxford University Press, 2010.

Pinney, Christopher. 'Sepia Mutiny: Colonial Photography and Its Others in India.' In *Feeling Photography*, edited by Elspeth Brown and Thy Phu, 71–92. Durham, NC: Duke University Press, 2014.

Rao, Velcheru Narayana. 'Print and Prose: Pundits, *Karanams*, and the East India Company in the Making of Modern Telugu'. In *India's Literary History: Essays on the Nineteenth Century*, edited by Stuart Blackburn and Vasudha Dalmia, 146–166. New Delhi: Permanent Black, 2004.

Richards, Thomas. *The Imperial Archive: Knowledge and the Fantasy of Empire*. London: Verso, 1993.

Roy, Anindyo. *Civility and Empire: Literature and Culture in British India, 1822–1922*. London: Routledge, 2005.

Teltscher, Kate. *India Inscribed: European and English Writing on India, 1600–1800*. Delhi: Oxford University Press, 1997.

Tobin, Beth Fowkes. *Picturing Imperial Power: Colonial Subjects in Eighteenth-Century British Painting*. Durham, NC: Duke University Press, 1999, 110–138.

Trivedi, Harish. *Colonial Transactions: English Literature and India*. Calcutta: Papyrus, 1993.

Viswanathan, Gauri. *Masks of Conquest: English Literary Studies and India*. London: Faber & Faber, 1990.

Webb, William Trego. *English Etiquette for Indian Gentlemen*. 5th ed. 1895. Calcutta: S.K. Lahiri, 1915.

Williamson, Thomas. *Oriental Field Sports*. London: W. Bulmer, 1808.

INTRODUCTION

The British, like other Europeans in Africa and Asian colonies, explained, defended and promoted their presence and action by presenting themselves in the role of the civilisers.

The abolition of *sati*, the temperance movement, the 'age of consent' campaign were social interventions, skirting close to religious interference. These were cast as a bounden duty of the Empire. When William Carey and the Serampore missionaries or T.B. Macaulay wrote their treatises, Minutes and reports advocating Christian proselytising or English education, they did so by pointing to the possible advantages to the colonised.

Macaulay's notorious dismissal of the Indian knowledge systems, cultures and languages was accompanied, as the 1835 Minute included here shows, by a view that English education would yet make good administrators and clerks of the colonised. Priscilla Chapman similarly saw English education as a key means of raising the always subjugated Indian woman. The issue of educating Indians of all castes, religions and faiths was a subset of the larger debate on social and 'moral' reform of the colonised. In this, the bigger debate surrounded proselytising, conversion and the propagation of the Christian faith among the Indians, and documents, such as Claudius Buchanan's and Alexander Duff's excerpted here, were instrumental in escalating the debate to the English Parliament, on occasion. In works of Irene Barnes, we also find accounts of the manner and mode through which missionaries and educationists embarked upon and engaged in the field, the battles they fought, the resistance they encountered and the commitment they brought to the field. W.S. Caine speaks eloquently of the need for a temperance movement in India. Stirckland surveys the voluntary associations and welfare work in the subcontinent. John Megaw highlights the major public health initiatives of the British government in India.

The 'civilisational mission' was a form of moral imperialism, proceeding from a sense of their (British) superiority and modernity, whether in education or religious beliefs, cultural practices or social norms. It was compounded by studies and writings that presented the colonised as primitives in need of salvation and rescue (see Volume 1). The archive demonstrates the power of stereotypes in the documents of the 'civilisational mission'.

ACKNOWLEDGEMENTS

The Raj has been a perennial favourite when it comes to research and writing, and I cannot remember a year when I did *not* do some 'Raj work'.

Chandra Sekhar of Bloomsbury was very receptive to the project idea, and has been incisive and encouraging when it came to subjects like the volumes' organisation, content and final form—to him, this project owes much.

I express my thanks to journals and anthologies, and their editors and reviewers whose comments have enabled me to sharpen my thoughts on the Raj-topic-of-the-moment. Among journals, I acknowledge: *South Asia, South Asian Review, Anglo-Saxonica* and *Asiatic*. Among the anthologies, I acknowledge *Ireland's Imperial Connections*; *The Edinburgh History of Reading*; *The English Renaissance, Orientalism, and the Idea of Asia*; *Cultural Histories of India*. To Debra Johanyak and Walter S. Lim, Rita Banerjee, Daniel Roberts and Jonathan Wright, Mary Hammond and Jonathan Rose, editors of these fabulous anthologies, many thanks for your invitation to contribute and the work you put into the volumes of which I am now a part.

To Kate Teltscher, whose work *India Inscribed* showed me where to go way back in the mid-1990s, I owe an intellectual debt of enormous proportions.

I am also grateful to publishers and editors at Penguin, Bloomsbury, Palgrave-Macmillan, Edinburgh University Press, Orient BlackSwan, Wiley-Blackwell and Routledge for their comments, suggestions and, above all, interest in this area and my contributions to it.

To Soma Ghosh, Librarian (English) at the Salar Jung Museum, Hyderabad, and her constant efforts, all undertaken with cheer and grace, to obtain materials when I have worked there, immeasurable gratitude.

Many books germinate in conversations with Anna Kurian, who is always enthusiastic about any Raj-work I do, especially if they are multivolume projects. For the constant-traveller role that you assay with such commitment, solidarity and affection, it is my privilege, Anna, to acknowledge you.

Thank you, Molly ('Chechu'), for enquiring lovingly about her 'little one'.

Nandana Dutta has been unceasing in her interest in my work, and her always gentle and loving urging to think in certain ways, even as she tries to catch up with her reading of what I publish. To your attention, insights and perspicacity, Nandana—much, much gratitude.

Professor K. Narayana Chandran established, for some of us willing ones, the standards in academic scholarship and publishing—that he sustains these standards even now, after four decades, is nothing short of the marvellous. To KNC's indomitable spirit of inquiry and work ethic, and showing us the way to do things, I am very grateful.

Friends who drop in 'WhatsAppingly', regularly, to check on me—Neelu, Bhalla, Ajeet, Kulsoom, Om, Archana, Ashish, Krishna Ram, Sai Jawahar, Savita, Vaishali, Soma and Zahid—thank you.

To Nandini, Pranav, my parents and parents-in-law, I owe unquantifiable gratitude, for never complaining at the volume of work I take on, my frequently distracted state of being and, more importantly, for creating an extraordinarily supportive environment.

And thank you, Shubha, for obtaining, wizard-like, essays and journal articles in minutes, and for your enthusiasm for my work.

To the works of P.G. Wodehouse, Agatha Christie, Stephen King, the comics around Batman—my regular reading—many of which unwittingly capture the horror, the abyss and the comedy of academia, I can never express enough gratitude.

It is a pleasure to thank Atul Nair who compiled many of the materials meticulously.

I am grateful to the Institution of Eminence (IoE) project's Professional Development Fund.

T.B. Macaulay

'Minute on English Education, 2nd February 1835'. *In Selections from Educational Records Part I, 1781–1839*, edited by H. Sharp. Calcutta: Government Printing, 1920.

Macaulay's Minute on Education, February 2, 1835

Minute by the Hon'ble T. B. Macaulay, dated the 2nd February 1835.

As it seems to be the opinion of some of the gentlemen who compose the Committee of Public Instruction that the course which they have hitherto pursued was strictly prescribed by the British Parliament in 1813 and as, if that opinion be correct, a legislative act will be necessary to warrant a change, I have thought it right to refrain from taking any part in the preparation of the adverse statements which are now before us, and to reserve what I had to say on the subject till it should come before me as a Member of the Council of India.

It does not appear to me that the Act of Parliament can by any art of contraction be made to bear the meaning which has been assigned to it. It contains nothing about the particular languages or sciences which are to be studied. A sum is set apart "for the revival and promotion of literature, and the encouragement of the learned natives of India, and for the introduction and promotion of a knowledge of the sciences among the inhabitants of the British territories." It is argued, or rather taken for granted, that by literature the Parliament can have meant only Arabic and Sanscrit literature; that they never would have given the honourable appellation of "a learned native" to a native who was familiar with the poetry of Milton, the metaphysics of Locke, and the physics of Newton; but that they meant to designate by that name only such persons as might have studied in the sacred books of the Hindoos all the uses of cusa-grass, and all the mysteries of absorption into the Deity. This does not appear to be a very satisfactory interpretation. To take a parallel case: Suppose that the Pacha of Egypt, a country once superior in knowledge to the nations of Europe, but now sunk far below them, were to appropriate a sum for the purpose "of reviving and promoting literature, and encouraging learned natives of Egypt," would any body infer that he meant the youth of his Pachalik to give years to the study of hieroglyphics, to search into all the doctrines disguised under the fable of Osiris, and to ascertain with all possible accuracy the ritual with which cats and onions were anciently adored? Would he be justly charged with inconsistency if, instead of employing his young subjects in deciphering obelisks, he were to order them to be instructed in the English and French languages, and in all the sciences to which those languages are the chief keys?

The words on which the supporters of the old system rely do not bear them out, and other words follow which seem to be quite decisive on the other side. This lakh of rupees is set apart not only for "reviving literature in India," the phrase on which their whole interpretation is founded, but also "for the introduction and promotion of a knowledge of the sciences among the inhabitants of the British territories"-words which are alone sufficient to authorize all the changes for which I contend.

If the Council agree in my construction no legislative act will be necessary. If they differ from me, I will propose a short act rescinding that I clause of the Charter of 1813 from which the difficulty arises.

The argument which I have been considering affects only the form of proceeding. But the admirers of the oriental system of education have used another argument, which, if we admit it to be valid, is decisive against all change. They conceive that the public faith is pledged to the present system, and that to alter the appropriation of any of the funds which have hitherto been spent in encouraging the study of Arabic and Sanscrit would be downright spoliation. It is not easy to understand by what process of reasoning they can have arrived at this conclusion. The grants which are made from the public purse for the encouragement of literature differ in no respect from the grants which are made from the same purse for other objects of real or supposed utility. We found a sanitarium on a spot which we suppose to be healthy. Do we thereby pledge ourselves to keep a sanitarium there if the result should not answer our expectations? We commence the erection of a pier. Is it a violation of the public faith to stop the works, if we afterwards see reason to believe that the building will be useless? The rights of property are undoubtedly sacred. But nothing endangers those rights so much as the practice, now unhappily too common, of attributing them to things to which they do not belong. Those who would impart to abuses the sanctity of property are in truth imparting to the institution of property the unpopularity and the fragility of abuses. If the Government has given to any person a formal assurance-nay, if the Government has excited in any person's mind a reasonable expectation-that he shall receive a certain income as a teacher or a learner of Sanscrit or Arabic, I would respect that person's pecuniary interests. I would rather err on the side of liberality to individuals than suffer the public faith to be called in question. But to talk of a Government pledging itself to teach certain languages and certain sciences, though those languages may become useless, though those sciences may be exploded, seems to me quite unmeaning. There is not a single word in any public instrument from which it can be inferred that the Indian Government ever intended to give any pledge on this subject, or ever considered the destination of these funds as unalterably fixed. But, had it been otherwise, I should have denied the competence of our predecessors to bind us by any pledge on such a subject. Suppose that a Government had in the last century enacted in the most solemn manner that all its subjects should, to the end of time, be inoculated for the small-pox, would that Government be bound to persist in the practice after Jenner's discovery? These promises of which nobody claims the performance, and from which nobody can grant a release, these vested rights which vest in nobody, this property without proprietors, this robbery which makes nobody poorer, may be comprehended by persons of higher faculties than mine. I consider this plea merely as a set form of words, regularly used both in England and in India, in defence of every abuse for which no other plea can be set up.

I hold this lakh of rupees to be quite at the disposal of the Governor-General in Council for the purpose of promoting learning in India in any way which may be thought most advisable. I hold his Lordship to be quite as free to direct that it shall no longer be employed in encouraging Arabic and Sanscrit, as he is to direct that the reward for killing tigers in Mysore shall be diminished, or that no more public money shall be expended on the chaunting at the cathedral.

We now come to the gist of the matter. We have a fund to be employed as Government shall direct for the intellectual improvement of the people of this country. The simple question is, what is the most useful way of employing it?

All parties seem to be agreed on one point, that the dialects commonly spoken among the natives of this part of India contain neither literary nor scientific information, and are moreover so poor and rude that, until they are enriched from some other quarter, it will not be easy to translate any valuable work into them. It seems to be admitted on all sides, that the intellectual improvement of those classes of the people who have the means of pursuing higher studies can at present be affected only by means of some language not vernacular amongst them.

What then shall that language be? One-half of the committee maintain that it should be the English. The other half strongly recommend the Arabic and Sanscrit. The whole question seems to me to be-which language is the best worth knowing?

I have no knowledge of either Sanscrit or Arabic. But I have done what I could to form a correct estimate of their value. I have read translations of the most celebrated Arabic and Sanscrit works. I have conversed, both here and at home, with men distinguished by their proficiency in the Eastern tongues. I am quite ready to take the oriental learning at the valuation of the orientalists themselves. I have never found one among them who could deny that a single shelf of a good European library was worth the whole native literature of India and Arabia. The intrinsic superiority of the Western literature is indeed fully admitted by those members of the committee who support the oriental plan of education.

It will hardly be disputed, I suppose, that the department of literature in which the Eastern writers stand highest is poetry. And I certainly never met with any orientalist who ventured to maintain that the Arabic and Sanscrit poetry could be compared to that of the great European nations. But when we pass from works of imagination to works in which facts are recorded and general principles investigated, the superiority of the Europeans becomes absolutely immeasurable. It is, I believe, no exaggeration to say that all the historical information which has been collected from all the books written in the Sanscrit language is less valuable than what may be found in the most paltry abridgments used at preparatory schools in England. In every branch of physical or moral philosophy, the relative position of the two nations is nearly the same.

How then stands the case? We have to educate a people who cannot at present be educated by means of their mother-tongue. We must teach them some foreign language. The claims of our own language it is hardly necessary to recapitulate. It stands pre-eminent even among the languages of the West. It abounds with works of imagination not inferior to the noblest which Greece has bequeathed to us,-with models of every species of eloquence,-with historical composition, which, considered merely as narratives, have seldom been surpassed, and which, considered as vehicles of ethical and political instruction, have never been equaled-with just and lively representations of human life and human nature,-with the most profound speculations on metaphysics, morals, government, jurisprudence, trade,-with full and correct information respecting every experimental science which tends to preserve the health, to increase the comfort, or to expand the intellect of man. Whoever knows that language has ready access to all the vast intellectual wealth which all the wisest nations of the earth have created and hoarded in the course of ninety generations. It may safely be said that the literature now extant in that language is of greater value than all the literature which three hundred years ago was extant in all the languages of the world together. Nor is this all. In India, English is the language spoken by the ruling class. It is spoken by the higher class of natives at the seats of Government. It is likely to become the language of commerce throughout the seas of the East. It is the language of two great European communities which are rising, the one in the south of Africa, the other in Australia,-communities which are every year becoming more important and more closely connected with our Indian empire. Whether we look at the intrinsic value of our literature, or at the particular situation of this country, we shall see the strongest reason to think that, of all foreign tongues, the English tongue is that which would be the most useful to our native subjects.

The question now before us is simply whether, when it is in our power to teach this language, we shall teach languages in which, by universal confession, there are no books on any subject which deserve to be compared to our own, whether, when we can teach European science, we shall teach systems which, by universal confession, wherever they differ from those of Europe differ for the worse, and whether, when we can patronize sound philosophy and true history, we shall countenance, at the public expense, medical doctrines which would disgrace an English farrier, astronomy which would move laughter in girls at an English boarding school, history abounding with kings thirty feet high and reigns thirty thousand years long, and geography made of seas of treacle and seas of butter.

We are not without experience to guide us. History furnishes several analogous cases, and they all teach the same lesson. There are, in modern times, to go no further, two memorable instances of a great impulse given to the mind of a whole society, of prejudices overthrown, of knowledge diffused, of taste purified, of arts and sciences planted in countries which had recently been ignorant and barbarous.

The first instance to which I refer is the great revival of letters among the Western nations at the close of the fifteenth and the beginning of the sixteenth century. At that time almost everything that was worth reading was contained in the writings of the ancient Greeks and Romans. Had our ancestors acted as the Committee of Public Instruction has hitherto noted, had they neglected the language of Thucydides and Plato, and the language of Cicero and Tacitus, had they confined their attention to the old dialects of our own island, had they printed nothing and taught nothing at the universities but chronicles in Anglo-Saxon and romances in Norman French,-would England ever have been what she now is? What the Greek and Latin were to the contemporaries of More and Ascham, our tongue is to the people of India. The literature of England is now more valuable than that of classical antiquity. I doubt whether the Sanscrit literature be as valuable as that of our Saxon and Norman progenitors. In some departments-in history for example-I am certain that it is much less so.

Another instance may be said to be still before our eyes. Within the last hundred and twenty years, a nation which had previously been in a state as barbarous as that in which our ancestors were before the Crusades has gradually emerged from the ignorance in which it was sunk, and has taken its place among civilized communities. I speak of Russia. There is now in that country a large educated class abounding with persons fit to serve the State in the highest functions, and in nowise inferior to the most accomplished men who adorn the best circles of Paris and London. There is reason to hope that this vast empire which, in the time of our grandfathers, was probably behind the Punjab, may in the time of our grandchildren, be pressing close on France and Britain in the career of improvement. And how was this change effected? Not by flattering national prejudices; not by feeding the mind of the young Muscovite with the old women's stories which his rude fathers had believed; not by filling his head with lying legends about St. Nicholas; not by encouraging him to study the great question, whether the world was or not created on the 13th of September; not by calling him "a learned native" when he had mastered all these points of knowledge; but by teaching him those foreign languages in which the greatest mass of information had been laid up, and thus putting all that information within his reach. The languages of western Europe civilised Russia. I cannot doubt that they will do for the Hindoo what they have done for the Tartar.

And what are the arguments against that course which seems to be alike recommended by theory and by experience? It is said that we ought to secure the co-operation of the native public, and that we can do this only by teaching Sanscrit and Arabic.

I can by no means admit that, when a nation of high intellectual attainments undertakes to superintend the education of a nation comparatively ignorant, the learners are absolutely to prescribe the course which is to be taken by the teachers. It is not necessary however to say anything on this subject. For it is proved by unanswerable evidence, that we are not at present securing the co-operation of the natives. It would be bad enough to consult their intellectual taste at the expense of their intellectual health. But we are consulting neither. We are withholding from them the learning which is palatable to them. We are forcing on them the mock learning which they nauseate.

This is proved by the fact that we are forced to pay our Arabic and Sanscrit students while those who learn English are willing to pay us. All the declamations in the world about the love and reverence of the natives for their sacred dialects will never, in the mind of any impartial person, outweigh this undisputed fact, that we cannot find in all our vast empire a single student who will let us teach him those dialects, unless we will pay him.

I have now before me the accounts of the Mudrassa for one month, the month of December, 1833. The Arabic students appear to have been seventy-seven in number. All receive stipends from the public. The whole amount paid to them is above 500 rupees a month. On the other side of the account stands the following item:

Deduct amount realized from the out-students of English for the months of May, June, and July last-103 rupees.

I have been told that it is merely from want of local experience that I am surprised at these phenomena, and that it is not the fashion for students in India to study at their own charges. This only confirms me in my opinions. Nothing is more certain than that it never can in any part of the world be necessary to pay men for doing what they think pleasant or profitable. India is no exception to this rule. The people of India do not require to be paid for eating rice when they are hungry, or for wearing woollen cloth in the cold season. To come nearer to the case before us:-The children who learn their letters and a little elementary arithmetic from the village schoolmaster are not paid by him. He is paid for teaching them. Why then is it necessary to pay people to learn Sanscrit and Arabic? Evidently because it is universally felt that the Sanscrit and Arabic are languages the knowledge of which does not compensate for the trouble of acquiring them. On all such subjects the state of the market is the detective test.

Other evidence is not wanting, if other evidence were required. A petition was presented last year to the committee by several ex-students of the Sanscrit College. The petitioners stated that they had studied in the college ten or twelve years, that they had made themselves acquainted with Hindoo literature and science, that they had received certificates of proficiency. And what is the fruit of all this? "Notwithstanding such testimonials," they say, "we have but little prospect of bettering our condition without the kind assistance of your honourable committee, the indifference with which we are generally looked upon by our countrymen leaving no hope of encouragement and assistance from them." They therefore beg that they may be recommended to the Governor-General for places under the Government-not places of high dignity or emolument, but such as may just enable them to exist. "We want means," they say, "for a decent living, and for our progressive improvement, which, however, we cannot obtain without the assistance of Government, by whom we have been educated and maintained from childhood." They conclude by representing very pathetically that they are sure that it was never the intention of Government, after behaving so liberally to them during their education, to abandon them to destitution and neglect.

I have been used to see petitions to Government for compensation. All those petitions, even the most unreasonable of them, proceeded on the supposition that some loss had been sustained, that some wrong had been inflicted. These are surely the first petitioners who ever demanded compensation for having been educated gratis, for having been supported by the public during twelve years, and then sent forth into the world well furnished with literature and science. They represent their education as an injury which gives them a claim on the Government for redress, as an injury for which the stipends paid to them during the infliction were a very inadequate compensation. And I doubt not that they are in the right. They have wasted the best years of life in learning what procures for them neither bread nor respect. Surely we might with advantage have saved the cost of making these persons useless and miserable. Surely, men may be brought up to be burdens to the public and objects of contempt to their neighbours at a somewhat smaller charge to the State. But such is our policy. We do not even stand neuter in the contest between truth and falsehood. We are not content to leave the natives to the influence of their own hereditary prejudices. To the natural difficulties which obstruct the progress of sound science in the East, we add great difficulties of our own making. Bounties and premiums, such as ought not to be given even for the propagation of truth, we lavish on false texts and false philosophy.

By acting thus we create the very evil which we fear. We are making that opposition which we do not find. What we spend on the Arabic and Sanscrit Colleges is not merely a dead loss to the cause of truth. It is bounty-money paid to raise up champions of error. It goes to form a nest not merely of helpless placehunters but of bigots prompted alike by passion and by interest to raise a cry against every useful scheme of education. If there should be any opposition among the natives to the change which I recommend, that opposition will be the effect of our own system. It will be headed by persons supported by our stipends and trained in our colleges. The longer we persevere in our present course, the more formidable will that opposition be. It will be every year reinforced by recruits whom we are paying. From the native society, left to itself, we have no difficulties to apprehend. All the murmuring will come from that oriental interest which we have, by artificial means, called into being and nursed into strength.

There is yet another fact which is alone sufficient to prove that the feeling of the native public, when left to itself, is not such as the supporters of the old system represent it to be. The committee have thought fit to lay out above a lakh of rupees in printing Arabic and Sanscrit books. Those books find no purchasers. It is very rarely that a single copy is disposed of. Twenty-three thousand volumes, most of them folios and quartos, fill the libraries or rather the lumber-rooms of this body. The committee contrive to get rid of some portion of their vast stock of oriental literature by giving books away. But they cannot give so fast as they print. About twenty thousand rupees a year are spent in adding fresh masses of waste paper to a hoard which, one should think, is already sufficiently ample. During the last three years about sixty thousand rupees have been expended in this manner. The sale of Arabic and Sanscrit books during those three years has not yielded quite one thousand rupees. In the meantime, the School Book Society is selling seven or eight thousand English volumes every year, and not only pays the expenses of printing but realizes a profit of twenty per cent. on its outlay.

The fact that the Hindoo law is to be learned chiefly from Sanscrit books, and the Mahometan law from Arabic books, has been much insisted on, but seems not to bear at all on the question. We are commanded by Parliament to ascertain and digest the laws of India. The assistance of a Law Commission has been given to us for that purpose. As soon as the Code is promulgated the Shasters and the Hedaya will be useless to a moonsiff or a Sudder Ameen. I hope and trust that, before the boys who are now entering at the Mudrassa and the Sanscrit College have completed their studies, this great work will be finished. It would be manifestly absurd to educate the rising generation with a view to a state of things which we mean to alter before they reach manhood.

But there is yet another argument which seems even more untenable. It is said that the Sanscrit and the Arabic are the languages in which the sacred books of a hundred millions of people are written, and that they are on that account entitled to peculiar encouragement. Assuredly it is the duty of the British Government in India to be not only tolerant but neutral on all religious questions. But to encourage the study of a literature, admitted to be of small intrinsic value, only because that literature inculcated the most serious errors on the most important subjects, is a course hardly reconcilable with reason, with morality, or even with that very neutrality which ought, as we all agree, to be sacredly preserved. It is confined that a language is barren of useful knowledge. We are to teach it because it is fruitful of monstrous superstitions. We are to teach false history, false astronomy, false medicine, because we find them in company with a false religion.

We abstain, and I trust shall always abstain, from giving any public encouragement to those who are engaged in the work of converting the natives to Christianity. And while we act thus, can we reasonably or decently bribe men, out of the revenues of the State, to waste their youth in learning how they are to purify themselves after touching an ass or what texts of the Vedas they are to repeat to expiate the crime of killing a goat?

It is taken for granted by the advocates of oriental learning that no native of this country can possibly attain more than a mere smattering of English. They do not attempt to prove this. But they perpetually insinuate it. They designate the education which their opponents recommend as a mere spelling-book education. They assume it as undeniable that the question is between a profound knowledge of Hindoo and Arabian literature and science on the one side, and superficial knowledge of the rudiments of English on the other. This is not merely an assumption, but an assumption contrary to all reason and experience. We know that foreigners of all nations do learn our language sufficiently to have access to all the most abstruse knowledge which it contains sufficiently to relish even the more delicate graces of our most idiomatic writers. There are in this very town natives who are quite competent to discuss political or scientific questions with fluency and precision in the English language. I have heard the very question on which I am now writing discussed by native gentlemen with a liberality and an intelligence which would do credit to any member of the Committee of Public Instruction. Indeed it is unusual to find, even in the literary circles of the Continent, any foreigner who can express himself in English with so much facility and correctness as we find in many Hindoos. Nobody, I suppose, will contend that English is so difficult to a Hindoo as Greek to an Englishman. Yet an intelligent English youth, in a much smaller number of years than our unfortunate pupils pass at the Sanscrit College, becomes able to read, to enjoy, and even to imitate not unhappily the compositions of the best Greek authors. Less than half the time which enables an English youth to read Herodotus and Sophocles ought to enable a Hindoo to read Hume and Milton.

To sum up what I have said. I think it clear that we are not fettered by the Act of Parliament of 1813, that we are not fettered by any pledge expressed or implied, that we are free to employ our funds as we choose, that we ought to employ them in teaching what is best worth knowing, that English is better worth knowing than Sanscrit or Arabic, that the natives are desirous to be taught English, and are not desirous to be taught Sanscrit or Arabic, that neither as the languages of law nor as the languages of religion have the Sanscrit and Arabic any peculiar claim to our encouragement, that it is possible to make natives of this country thoroughly good English scholars, and that to this end our efforts ought to be directed.

In one point I fully agree with the gentlemen to whose general views I am opposed. I feel with them that it is impossible for us, with our limited means, to attempt to educate the body of the people. We must at present do our best to form a class who may be interpreters between us and the millions whom we govern, -a class of persons Indian in blood and colour, but English in tastes, in opinions, in morals and in intellect. To that class we may leave it to refine the vernacular dialects of the country, to enrich those dialects with terms of science borrowed from the Western nomenclature, and to render them by degrees fit vehicles for conveying knowledge to the great mass of the population.

I would strictly respect all existing interests. I would deal even generously with all individuals who have had fair reason to expect a pecuniary provision. But I would strike at the root of the bad system which has hitherto been fostered by us. I would at once stop the printing of Arabic and Sanscrit books. I would abolish the Mudrassa and the Sanscrit College at Calcutta. Benares is the great seat of Brahminical learning; Delhi of Arabic learning. If we retain the Sanscrit College at Bonares and the Mahometan College at Delhi we do enough and much more than enough in my opinion, for the Eastern languages. If the Benares and Delhi Colleges should be retained, I would at least recommend that no stipends shall be given to any students who may hereafter repair thither, but that the people shall be left to make their own choice between the rival systems of education without being bribed by us to learn what they have no desire to know. The funds which would thus be placed at our disposal would enable us to give larger encouragement to the Hindoo College at Calcutta, and establish in the principal cities throughout the Presidencies of Fort William and Agra schools in which the English language might be well and thoroughly taught.

If the decision of His Lordship in Council should be such as I anticipate, I shall enter on the performance of my duties with the greatest zeal and alacrity. If, on the other hand, it be the opinion of the Government that the present system ought to remain unchanged, I beg that I may be permitted to retire from the chair of the Committee. I feel that I could not be of the smallest use there. I feel also that I should be lending my countenance to what I firmly believe to be a mere delusion. I believe that the present system tends not to accelerate the progress of truth but to delay the natural death of expiring errors. I conceive that we have at present no right to the respectable name of a Board of Public Instruction. We are a Board for wasting the public money, for printing books which are of less value than the paper on which they are printed was while it was blank-for giving artificial encouragement to absurd history, absurd metaphysics, absurd physics, absurd theology-for raising up a breed of scholars who find their scholarship an incumbrance and blemish, who live on the public while they are receiving their education, and whose education is so utterly useless to them that, when they have received it, they must either starve or live on the public all the rest of their lives. Entertaining these opinions, I am naturally desirous to decline all share in the responsibility of a body which, unless it alters its whole mode of proceedings, I must consider, not merely as useless, but as positively noxious.

Claudius Buchanan

An Apology for Promoting Christianity in India. London: T. Cadell and W. Davies, 1813.

LETTER AND MEMORIAL,

TO

LORD MINTO.

LETTER.

TO THE RIGHT HONOURABLE LORD MINTO,
&c. &c. &c.

MY LORD,

I BEG leave respectfully to submit to your Lordship some particulars regarding the present state of the Christian Religion in Bengal, which I have thought it my duty to communicate for your Lordship's information at this time.

I trust your Lordship will do me the justice to believe that it is with the utmost reluctance I trouble your Lordship with a letter on such a subject [illegible] soon after your entrance on this government, when [illegible] yet few, if any, of the circumstances noticed in it can have come to your Lordship's knowledge.

I have no other view in soliciting your Lordship's attention to them, but the advancement of learning and religion. Perhaps [illegible] one has addressed your Lordship on the subject since your arrival; and there are certainly many particulars regarding their present state, which it is of importance your Lordship should know.

Being about to leave India, I feared lest I should hereafter reproach myself, if I withheld any thing at this time which I conceived might be useful, particularly as I have been further encouraged to address your Lordship, by your Lordship's known condescension in receiving any communications which are honestly intended.

I have the honour to be, my Lord,

With much respect,

Your most obedient, humble servant,

(Signed) C. BUCHANAN.

Calcutta,
9th November, 1807.

MEMORIAL.

TO THE RIGHT HON. GILBERT, LORD MINTO, GOVERNOR-GENERAL, &c. &c. &c.

MY LORD,

1. I HAD the honour to receive a letter from the Chief Secretary to the Government, under date the 11th September, desiring that I would submit, for the inspection of Government, the manuscript of some Sermons on the Prophecies which I intended to publish. I shall willingly submit these discourses to your Lordship's perusal, and shall be happy to receive such observations [illegible] them [illegible] your Lordship's learning and candour may suggest; but I cannot submit them to the judgment of the Officers of the Government. My reasons for declining to comply with the wishes of Government in this respect, it is incumbent on me to state; and I feel confident your Lordship will consider them to be satisfactory.

2. It will not have escaped your Lordship's observation, even in the short period since your arri-

val, that some of the officers of your Lordship's government do not manifest any zeal for promoting the knowledge of the Christian Religion in India: they consider that a zeal in this respect would not be consonant to a wise and prudent policy. I am willing to believe that they advise according to the best of their judgment; but a principle pure and just in itself, if it be not tenderly exercised in reference to other important obligations, may become extravagant or pernicious. For instance, not to promote Christianity may, in certain circumstances, be prudent; but to repress Christianity will not, I think, in any case be defended. It is not necessary to observe to your Lordship how much the minds of Europeans assimilate to the native character after a long residence in this country, and how difficult it is for men, even of good sense and honest intentions, while involved in the mist of this prejudice, to view the Christian religion in the true light.

3. During the administration of the Marquis Wellesley, the spirit of promoting learning and religion in India was general and ardent; but after the departure of that nobleman, a great revolution took place. A spirit, directly adverse to the diffusion of religion in India, most unexpectedly broke forth, just as if it had been confined by his presence. This spirit appeared long before

the insurrection in Vellore. I mention this, lest your Lordship should suppose that it originated with that event; for I understood that the "Massacre at Vellore" has been unaccountably adduced as some sanction to the principle of opposing the progress of the Christian Religion in Bengal. I had opportunities of judging of the causes of that event, which were peculiar. I was in the vicinity of the place at the time; I travelled for two months immediately afterwards in the provinces adjacent, with the sanction of Government; and I heard the evidence of Christians, Mahometans, and Hindoos, on the subject. That the insurrection at Vellore had no connection with the Christian Religion, directly or indirectly, immediately or remotely, is a truth which is capable of demonstration.

4. The spirit so hostile to the progress of Christianity in India, appeared first in operation about two years ago, and has been acquiring strength ever since. It has exhibited itself in a series of acts, the recital of which will sufficiently illustrate to your Lordship the temper of mind which produced them. These acts are, however, not to be considered as the official and acknowledged measures of the respectable person, who preceded your Lordship in the government. Sir George Barlow has often expressed his approbation of the means

used for the diffusion of Christianity in India, and he sincerely desires its success. These measures have not been generally considered as the offspring of his unbiassed judgment. Besides, most of them are extra official, and with some of them he is perhaps yet unacquainted. They will probably appear to your Lordship to have been dictated by a timorous policy, proceeding from minds somewhat agitated by the responsibility of a weighty empire, viewing at the same time Christianity as an innovation in India, and magnifying that innovation, perhaps, into a revolution. The acts which have plainly manifested this alarm are many. It will suffice to notice to your Lordship the four following:

5. First. The withdrawing the patronage of Government from the translation of the Holy Scriptures into the Oriental Tongues.

The translation of the Scriptures had commenced in the College of Fort William, at the expense of Government. When the Honourable the Court of Directors directed a reduction of the expenses of that institution, it was resolved to make provision for the continuation of the translation of the Scriptures by public subscription, and to exonerate the Government entirely. It was accordingly proposed that a Committee of the College and of others should superintend the translations, and controul the expenditure. This measure had been recommended by certain of the bishops and by some noble persons in England, who wished to aid us in the translation of the Scriptures; and the countenance of the College was merely desired, with the view that the important work might be conducted strictly in the principles of the national church, and not fall entirely into the hands of dissenters, as it has since done. Your Lordship will be surprised to hear that this proposition was rejected. Government withdrew its patronage from the work entirely, and even refused to give its countenance to the subscription. The immediate consequences of this unexpected blow was the loss of ample funds; for there appeared at the time, throughout all India, a disposition to encourage a literary undertaking which was deemed so honourable to the nation.

Considering the difficulty of obtaining fit instruments for the conduct of such a work, the religious and moral importance of the work itself, and its advantages to the general interests of Oriental Literature, your Lordship will believe, that this forfeiture of public encouragement, under such auspicious circumstances, has ever been viewed with regret by the friends of learning and of religion in Europe and in India.

This disappointment, however, has had one favourable result; it accelerated the establishment of "the Christian Institution in the East*," which carries the translation of the Scriptures, in some

---

* Early in 1806, in the view of the Translations of the Scriptures ceasing in the College of Fort William, Dr. Buchanan resolved to devote whatever influence he possessed in his official character ■ Vice-Provost of the College, to the aid of the Translations in the hands of the Baptist Missionaries, and to endeavour to excite ■ much of public interest in their favour as possible. For this purpose, he drew up "Proposals for ■ Subscription for translating the Holy "Scriptures into the following Oriental Languages; *Shanscrit, Bengalee, Hindoostanee, Persian, Mahratta, Guzerattee, Orissa, Carnata, Telinga, Burmah, Assam, Bootan, Tibet, Malay*, and *Chinese*;"— containing a prospectus of Indian versions, and observations on the practicability of the general design: signed by the nine Baptist Missionaries, and dated, "Mission House, Serampore, March 1806."—That paper was composed entirely by Dr. Buchanan, part of it from materials furnished by the Missionaries. But ■ it was apprehended the name "Baptist" might not be auspicious to the design, in the general view of the public, Dr. Buchanan did not admit that word, but designated them "Protestant Missionaries in Bengal;" ■ it stands in the proposals. Copies were distributed liberally in India and in England. To some of those distributed in England ■ prefixed ■ frontispiece representing ■ Hindoo receiving the Bible, and "bending to the Christian Faith." Copies were transmitted to almost the whole of the principal civil officers, and to many of the military officers in the Honourable Company's service throughout Hindostan, from Delhi to Travancore ■ many of whom had never heard of the Serampore Mission

of the languages, into regions far beyond the controul of the Bengal Government.

---

before. Dr. Buchanan obtained permission, at the same time, to send the proposals, in his official character as Vice-Provost of the College, free of expense, to all parts of the empire; and he accompanied them, in most instances, with a letter from himself. The design received encouragement from every quarter; and a sum of about 1600*l*. was soon raised for the translations; to which the late Rev. David Brown contributed 250*l*.

The concurrence of the public was the more easily obtained from its being implied in the proposals that the undertaking would enjoy the countenance of the College. That expectation was expressed in the following terms:

"Part XI. Our hope of success in this great undertaking depends chiefly on the patronage of the College of Fort William. To that institution we are much indebted for the progress we have already made. Oriental translation has become comparatively easy, in consequence of our having the aid of those learned men from distant provinces in Asia, who have assembled, during the period of the last six years, at that great emporium of Eastern Letters. These intelligent strangers voluntarily engage with us in translating the Scriptures into their respective languages; and they do not conceal their admiration of the sublime doctrine, pure precept, and Divine eloquence of the word of God. The plan of these translations was sanctioned at an early period by the Most Noble the Marquis Wellesley, the great patron of useful learning. To give the Christian Scriptures to the inhabitants of Asia is indeed a work which every man, who believes these Scriptures to be from God, will approve. In Hindostan alone, there is

"5. Second. Attempting to suppress the translation of the Scriptures.

" a great variety of religions; and there are some tribes " which have no certain cast or religion at all. To render " the revealed religion accessible to men who 'desire' it; " to open its eternal sanctions, and display its pure morals " to those who 'seek a religion;' is to fulfil the sacred duty " of a Christian people, and accords well with the humane " and generous spirit of the English nation.

" XII. It may also be expected, that the design will be " generally encouraged, on the ground of its promoting the " diffusion of Oriental Literature, and affording new facili- " ties to Europeans in obtaining a knowledge of the various " languages of this great empire. With every translation of " the Scriptures into a new language, it is intended to give " a grammar of that language, if none already exist.

" XIII. A copy of these Proposals has been forwarded to " the British Ambassador at Petersburg, with a request that " he would submit them to his Majesty the Emperor of all " the Russias; some of the languages above-mentioned be- " ing spoken in regions bordering on the territories of his " Majesty."

Although the Government of Bengal withdrew its patronage, most of the individuals in every part of India whose support was then secured, being satisfied that the simple translation of the Holy Scriptures must ever be a measure utterly devoid of objection, have continued steady friends to the undertaking to this day.

Afterwards, when Dr. Buchanan visited the southern regions of India, and had witnessed the triumph of Christianity on the one hand, and the horrors of Paganism on the other, he conceived the design of an institution of a more general nature for Oriental Illumination, than that confined to Ben-

An attempt was next made to suppress the translation of the Scriptures entirely, and this attempt had almost succeeded.

---

gal. [See his meditation on the banks of the Chilka Lake, on a Sunday morning, in view of the tower of Juggernaut, —Christian Researches, p. 142.] And on his return to Calcutta in the following year, he proposed to the Baptist Mission, that the different societies and individuals in India, engaged in translating the Scriptures, should associate (merely in that character) under the name of "The Christian Institution in the East," or the "British Propaganda;" in order that their operations might have the appearance of being national and not sectarian; and that thus they might be able to vie with the "Romish Propaganda," whose fame is yet alive in Asia. It was proposed that the Missionary pursuits, properly so called, and the individual establishments of each society should remain peculiar and private as before; but that the translators of the Scriptures should act in concert, and maintain an amicable correspondence with each other, under the general superintendance of the Rev. Mr. Brown, Provost of the College of Fort William, who had formerly, in discharge of his office as Provost, superintended the translations of the Scriptures in the College; and would continue to be the organ of communication to Government, and be responsible for the views and proceedings of the general society. This proposition the Baptist Society declined; and in consequence, the proposed of "Christian Institution" was but partially assumed. The other branches, nevertheless, were generally associated; and the Rev. Mr. Brown, superintended those branches of the department of Scriptural Translation, as they came suc-

To suppress the translation of the Scriptures, is to suppress the Scriptures. I can make no further observation on this, in addressing your Lordship.

7. Third. Suppressing the encomium of the Hon. the Court of Directors, on their venerable missionary the Rev. Mr. Swartz.

The Honourable Court had sent out to Fort

---

cessively into operation, to the day of his death, viz. the Rev. Henry Martyn and his co-adjutors Sabat and Mirza Fitrut, Translators of the *Hindoostanee* and *Arabic*, at Cawnpore; Messrs. Cran and Desgranges, translators of the *Telinga*, at Visagapatam; Thomas Jarrett, Esq. translator of the Sumatra or Western *Malay*, at Madras *: the Syrian Bishop and his priests, translators of the *Malay-alim*, at Travancore; Sebastiani, translator of the *Persian*, at Calcutta; and Dr. Leyden of the College of Fort William, translator of the *Pushtu*, *Maldivian*, *Baloch*, *Macassar*, and *Bugis* languages. Mr. Brown also opened a correspondence with Tanjore, Tranquebar, and Columbo, concerning editions of the Scriptures in the *Tamul* and *Cingalese*.

Exclusive of the 1600*l.* above-mentioned [illegible] have been subscribed for translations by the Baptist Missionaries, Dr. Buchanan had put down his [illegible] for 6000 rupees, 620l.; but after his return from visiting the Christians in Travancore and other places, he withdrew his subscription from the Northern Mission, which [illegible] now well patronised, and applied it to similar objects [illegible] the South where it [illegible] most wanted.

* Dr. Buchanan does not know whether Mr. Jarrett continued to prosecute the translation after he left India.

St. George ■ marble monument, to be erected in the church of St. Mary, to the memory of Mr. Swartz, inscribed with a suitable epitaph ; and they announced it, in their general letter, dated 29th October 1806, as a testimony of the deep sense they entertained of his transcendant merit, of his unwearied labours in the cause of religion and piety, and of his public services at Tanjore, where the influence of his name and character was for a long course of years productive of important benefits to the Company. The Honourable Court further adds :—" On no subject has the Court of " Directors been more unanimous, than in their " anxious desire to perpetuate the memory of this " eminent person, and to excite in others an emu-" lation of his great example." They direct, finally, that " translations shall be made of the " epitaph into the country languages, and publish-" ed at Madras, and that the native inhabitants " shall be encouraged to view the monument."

The Christians in Bengal were of course rejoiced to hear of the honourable testimony to the apostolic Swartz, and they expected that it would be acknowledged here, ■ at Fort St. George and Bombay ; but they were disappointed ; there was no recognition of the venerable Missionary in Bengal. The epitaph was not inserted in the Calcutta Gazette, nor was the slightest notice taken of the circumstance. And lest it might be supposed that it was omitted by accident, the official notice of the Governor in Council at Fort St. George, which appeared subsequently, relative to the day of commemoration, was also suppressed.

But what followed was yet more painful. Your Lordship will judge of the feelings of the Christians in this place, when they read, in the Government Gazette of the week following, an article whose obvious tendency was to bring the labours and character of the Christian Missionary into contempt *. Thus, while the Honourable the East India Company were adorning the sepulchres of their Missionaries and embalming their memory in the South, their own servants were treating the character with indignity in the North. We were at first alarmed, lest this might be the signal for the other papers to commence an attack on the humble and defenceless Missionaries; but we were happy to find, that not one of the seven papers of this Presidency followed the example of the official Gazette.

---

* The Mission to Greenland and Labrador, whose civilizing efficiency on the rude inhabitants of those regions has long been a theme of admiration to the Christian world, is held forth in that paper to public ridicule; and the simple narrative of the pious well-meaning Missionaries, is declared to "exhibit a degree of canting fanaticism well worthy of the followers of Cromwell."—Calcutta Gazette, 17th September, 1807.

As it is not probable that any of the particulars above-mentioned, have as yet come to your Lordship's knowledge, I beg leave to refer your Lordship to the enclosed printed paper (A) published by the authority of the Government of Fort St. George.

8. Fourth. Restraining the Protestant Missionaries in Bengal, from the exercise of their functions, and establishing an Imprimatur for theological works.

Men's minds were prepared, by the preceding circumstances, to expect little indulgence to Missionaries, but they were certainly not prepared to expect the event which followed.

The success of the Protestant Mission in Bengal had long been a source of uneasiness to those officers of Government who do not think it right to convert the natives. Some of the native Moonshees attached to the public offices, well knowing, from long acquaintance, their masters' sentiments on this subject, have not failed from time to time to urge them to countenance their petitions, and to lend their voice in accusing the Missionaries. Some clamour of this kind was raised at two different times within the last seven years; but it passed away without offence to the Christian Religion. The complaint of the Moonshees against the Missionaries, on the present occasion, is not, I understand, [illegible] serious as the former: they complain, that the Missionaries have, in a certain paper, "applied abusive epithets to Mahomet." The Missionaries certainly mistake the proper method of convincing the minds of men, if they use epithets of abuse; the successful method of preaching is by argument and affectionate address; and I presume this has been their general method during the fourteen years of their mission, else we cannot suppose their labours would have been followed with [illegible] much success.

At the same time, Christian Teachers are not to speak with reverence or courtesy of Juggernaut or Mahomet: they must speak [illegible] the Scriptures speak; that is, of false gods [illegible] false gods, and of [illegible] lying prophet [illegible] [illegible] lying prophet. The Mahometans apply abusive epiphets and vulgar curses to the idolatry of the Hindoos and to the faith of Christians, and these epithets are contained in books; and Government might, on the same principle, have been assailed with the petitions of Christians and Hindoos against the Mahometans. If the natives choose to go to hear the preaching or to read the books of the Missionaries, it is their pleasure [illegible] do so—it is no concern of Government. These poor Missionaries [illegible] not official characters: they have no power, no authority, no riches; and this the natives well know. They are like the first Apostles, contemned and despised by all casts; and if they are bereaved of the countenance of their own Government, they are bereaved indeed.

The complaint, however, of the Mahometans has produced a very serious event. The Protestant Missionaries in Bengal were prohibited, by order of Government dated 8th September last, from preaching to the natives *.

The Protestant Mission being situated at Serampore, a town belonging to the King of Denmark, the English Government requested the Danish Governor to give up the Mission Press, and ordered the Missionaries to remove to Calcutta. The Danish Governor resisted this demand, on the plea of the sovereignty of his nation †; and the English Government revoked their requisition. The English Government then issued an order prohibiting the Missionaries from printing

* It was generally understood that the former administration were unwilling to encounter the public odium of accomplishing this measure; and that, by pressing it with a serious countenance on Lord Minto immediately on his arrival, they surprised the Governor-general.

† Dr. Buchanan was misinformed in this particular. The Danish Governor did not, it seems, resist the demand, on the plea of the sovereignty of his nation, although he might have so done if it had pleased him; but he solicited the revocation of the demand, on the ground of "the distress to which the Missionaries would be exposed by the English Government's exacting a compliance with it," and on the ground of the convenience of the press to the Danish Government.

any books, "directed to the object of converting "the natives to Christianity." On this a question was proposed officially to the British Government by the Danish Governor; a question which your Lordship will be concerned to think should ever have been necessary. It was this: "Whether, among the books prohibited by the "British Government, the Bible in the Bengalee language was included?" The answer to this question your Lordship will read with yet more concern. It was the following: "We are not "aware of any objection to the promulgation of "the Scriptures in the Bengalee language, unaccompanied by any comments on the religions of "the country:" that is, the English Government were not "aware that there was any objection to "the publication of the Bible, yet they were not "certain." At all events, it must have "no com-"ment on the religions of the country:" that is, it must not be said of the Bible—"This is the word "of the true God, and more worthy of belief than "the Veda of Brahma:" nor must any illustration of its truth be noticed by reference to the Hindoo doctrines; for instance, by appealing to their own ideas of a Trinity, of an atonement, and of the "man twice born."

After some consideration, the English Government qualified (but did not revoke) their prohibition respecting works "directed to the object of a converting the natives," and informed the Missionaries officially that, "whatever they printed for "the future, must be submitted to the inspection "of the officers of Government:" and here the matter ended. An official Imprimatur is established for the theological works of the Protestant Missionaries; and preaching to the natives, beyond the limits of the Danish town, is entirely prohibited: and this, of course, amounts to nearly a total suppression of the Mission.

The chief inconvenience of the Imprimatur imposed is, not that religious books shall be submitted to the officers of Government, but that they must be submitted to the "native" officers of Government. If, indeed, the Christian officers of Government understood the Bengalee, Arabic, Orissa, Mahratta, and Chinese languages, then might the Missionaries expect that Christians would revise their works; but a Hindoo must revise the Bengalee, and a Mahometan the Arabic. Those very Mahometans who impeached the Missionaries in the first instance will necessarily be employed next to revise their theology. Was it ever heard that a Hindoo or a Mahometan gave a candid judgment of a Christian book? They will, of course, obliterate all passages which offend their own superstitions, and particularly those quotations from Scripture which speak of lying prophets, or the sin of idolatry.

I now beg leave to request your Lordship's attention to the plea on which these proceedings against the Protestant Missionaries have been grounded. It is this; "that the public faith has "been pledged to leave the natives in the undis-"turbed exercise of their religions." This is a proper pledge of our Legislature. It is proper not to disturb the natives in the exercise of their religion; nor has this pledge ever been broken, directly or indirectly. It is proper not to interfere with, or by violence to prevent, the superstition of the natives, if not criminal in itself, or affecting the public peace. But if, by the expression, "not "disturbing the natives in the exercise of their re-"ligion," be meant that "we are not to use means "for diffusing the knowledge of Christianity "among them," then it is to be observed, that this pledge has been violated by every Government in India, and has been systematically broken by the Honourable the East India Company from the year 1698 to the present time. The fact is, they have pledged themselves to a conduct just the reverse. The East India Company hold this country by a Charter, which expressly stipulates that they shall use means to instruct the Gentoos, &c. in the Christian Religion. (William III. 15th September 1698.) And this stipulation is in perfect accordance with their pledge of not disturbing the natives in the exercise of their superstitions by force, inasmuch as it is a very different thing to apply arguments to the mind and to inflict wounds on the body. It is their duty to civilize their barbarous subjects, and to teach them humanity, and for that purpose to address their understandings and their affections. At the same time, it is their duty not to disturb the exercise of their superstition by compulsory acts; and the Legislature has stipulated for the performance of both duties; and the first duty is [illegible] positive [illegible] the second. They first stipulate to do good, and they next stipulate not to do evil; and in consequence of this stipulation, the Honourable Company have constantly aided the Christian Missions in India; and at this time, they devote a considerable sum annually to their support. The Protestant Mission in Bengal commenced in 1758. The Honourable Company's ships brought out the annual supplies for this Mission, and before the year 1770, religious tracts were translated into the Bengalee language; and Hindoo Christians preached to their countrymen, in the time of Hastings, in the town of Calcutta. This Mission continued its labours till about the year 1790, when the supply of Missionaries from Europe failed. It was succeeded by the present Mission at Serampore in 1793.

The Calcutta mission [illegible] of extensive use in disseminating Christian principles through Northern India. They sent Arabic New Testaments to the court of Shah Allum, the Mahomedan King of Hindostan, then resident at Allahabad. The priests of his Majesty returned their thanks to the Missionaries, and requested that "the supply might be continued." It was continued for a time, and an investment of Arabic Bibles is soon expected, under the sanction of the Honourable Company, for a similar purpose. Little of the influence of Christianity in India has come, as yet, to the knowledge of the public. Englishmen in general know as little of the state of Christianity in India, as of the state of Hinduism. Two Christian Missions were at the same period tolerated by Shah Allum; one of which had existed since the time of Akbar the Great, and both of which exist unto this day.

At Seringapatam, under Hyder Sultaun the Mahomedan Prince of Mysore, the most complete toleration was permitted. In the Appendix to the enclosed pamphlet, your Lordship will see with what ardour the preaching of Swartz was received at Seringapatam, and how the noble Mahometans and Hindoos desired to learn from him what was the "right prayer." Romish Missions were tolerated by Hyder at the same time. Tippoo Sultaun was more intolerant than his father. He was at times a persecutor; yet he did not quench Christianity; and Missions now flourish in various parts of the Mysore country.

After these authorities, we certainly shall not refer to the Mahomedan Moonshees in Calcutta, for their opinion on the general relations of religious toleration in India.

I do not know whether your Lordship has been informed, that there are two Roman Catholic Missions in Bengal and the provinces adjacent. They have existed for a long period of time, and have been tolerated by the Mahomedan, Hindoo, Scik, Nepaul, and Tibet Governments. They have preached and published what they pleased, without any official restriction that we have ever heard of; and they now continue to follow their functions under the protection of the English Government, while the Protestant Missionaries are restrained and their theology is subjected to an official licence.

The proceedings against the Protestant Mission will naturally be supposed at home to have been called forth by some public commotion in Bengal, or by the bad moral character of the Missionaries. As to the first, they will be happy to hear, that we are now, and long have been, in a state of almost torpid tranquillity; and as to the character of the Missionaries, the Government has acknowledged them to be men of quiet demeanour, of pious intentions, and as deserving countenance and respect

vernments to let Christianity alone. In the annals of the British Administration in India, has there been no instance of the suppression of ■ Christian Mission. Our empire here subsists by the discrepancy of religious opinion. It is not good policy to strengthen the Hindoo Religion, or to strengthen the Mahomedan Religion; but it is good policy to strengthen the Christian Religion, because it is as yet the weakest. It is certainly our duty not to oppose it; for if this counsel "be "of God, we cannot resist it." And it would now be as easy to oppose the rushing of the BORE into the river Ganges, as to oppose the entrance of Christianity into the province of Bengal*.

9. After the perusal of the foregoing pages, your Lordship will be prepared to understand the cause of the late alarm regarding the Prophecies; not ■ public alarm indeed, but the alarm of some of the officers of your Lordship's government.

Having had occasion lately to preach a series of discourses on the Christian Prophecies, in the

---

■ The BORE is the rapid influx of the tide of the ocean into the Ganges. That river is wide at the mouth; but suddenly narrowing, the accumulated waters seek their level, and run forward in ■ continued billow, with ■ mighty rushing noise, ■ hundred miles up ■ country.

Presidency Church, some of the congregation expressed a wish that I would permit them to be printed, observing, that they had before made a similar request without effect; but as I was now about to return to Europe, they hoped I would bequeath to them these few discourses.

When it was understood by the officers of Government, that the sermons on the prophecies were to be published, they were alarmed:—your Lordship will scarcely divine the cause—it was this:—It seems these prophecies declare, "that "all nations shall be converted to the religion of "Christ." But if this be true, it was argued, What bad news to the Mahomedans and the Hindoos! In short, the advertisement announcing the intended publication of the Prophecies, which was sent to the Government Gazette, was suppressed; the advertisement itself was delivered in with trepidation to Government, and an order was immediately issued to the printers of the other papers, forbidding them to publish the alarming notice. In consequence of this order, it has been publicly understood that the Christian Prophecies are suppressed by authority.

I now beg leave to submit it to your Lordship's judgment, whether, in the view of the temper of mind displayed above, it would be proper in me to subject my compositions to the opinion and revision of the officers of your Lordship's government. Might there not be some danger in committing the Christian Prophecies to be altered and new-modelled by men who favour the disciples of Mahomet and Brahma? I incline not to commit them to the hands of those officers, from another consideration: it would be a bad precedent. I would not that it should be thought, that any where in the British dominions, there exists any thing like a civil inquisition into matters purely religious.

It is now nearly two months since I received the letter from Government on this matter, and I have not yet communicated my intentions. I now beg leave to inform your Lordship, that I do not wish to give Government any unnecessary offence. I shall not publish the Prophecies.

At the same time I beg leave most respectfully to assure your Lordship, that I am not in any way disappointed by the interference of Government on this occasion. The supposed suppression of the Christian Prophecies has produced the consequence that might be expected. The public curiosity has been greatly excited to see these Prophecies; and to draw the attention of men to the Divine Predictions, could be the only object I had in view in noticing them in the course of my public ministry. Another consequence will probably be; the Prophecies will be translated into the languages of the East, and thus pave the way, as has sometimes happened, for their own fulfilment.

10. Your Lordship will be enabled better to understand the real nature of this alarm regarding the Prophecies, when you are informed of the alarm which was excited about half a year before your Lordship's arrival, by the ancient "Christian Tablets."

In consequence of the inquiries, sanctioned by the Marquis Wellesley, into the history and literature of the Syrian Christians of Travancore, some ancient Manuscripts were announced, and also certain "Brass Tablets" of great antiquity, containing the privileges of these ancient Christians, asserting their rights of nobility, and declaring withal that they had a King. Your Lordship can hardly conceive the apprehensions which were excited by this discovery, in the minds of those who have been lately alarmed by the Prophecies. Even at the first, it was accounted an ominous mission to go "to rake up the ashes of Christianity", in the very midst of the Hindoos. But when it was announced that there were "glowing embers," nothing less seemed to be expected than that all Hindostan would shortly be "in a flame." For if it was true that Christianity once flourished in Hindostan, it followed that it might flourish again.

It was devoutly wished "that these Christian Tablets might sink to the bottom of the sea," and even the curiosity of the Hindoo Antiquaries was quenched in this horror of Christianity*.

That your Lordship may be assured that this alarm was real, and not fictitious, it is only necessary to add, that when the article of literary intelligence published in the Bombay Gazette, containing the account of these ancient Christians†, and of these "brass plates" (which account [illegible] certainly interesting [illegible] the Christian world in general, and to men of letters in particular,) arrived at Calcutta, it was suppressed, by authority, [illegible] something dangerous to the State; and the Bishop of Llandaff's Letter on the Civilization of India‡ had nearly shared the same fate.

11. It appearing from the recent events above noticed, that the diffusion of Christianity in Bengal is plainly obnoxious to some of the officers of Government, serious apprehensions are now en-

---

* These brass tablets are [illegible] deposited in the public library of the University of Cambridge.

† It had been previously published in the Bombay Gazette, by which means it reached Europe. It [illegible] published afterwards in England by the late Bishop of London.

‡ See Christian Researches, at conclusion.

tertained, that the attempt to suppress the translation of the Scriptures will be renewed. I cannot believe that the attempt will be made during your Lordship's administration. If, however, any sinister event should afford a pretext for reviving it, I humbly request that the Chinese Translation of the Scriptures may be spared. Suffer me, my Lord, to intercede for the Chinese. There are three English youths, who have been for two years past under the tuition of the Chinese Professor and his two Chinese Assistants, and they have now acquired ■ very considerable proficiency in the Chinese Language; and it is my intention to call them to England for public purposes, in three years hence, if their studies be not interrupted. This Class has been organized and maintained at ■ great expense. It is the only regular Chinese Class in the world, out of the limits of the Chinese Empire; and it will probably be the source of the first regular instruction in the Chinese Language in Great Britain*.

---

* The expense was upwards of 1300*l*. The Chinese Professor, Mr. Lassar, ■■■ originally engaged to superintend the Class at Serampore, by Dr. Buchanan, and was maintained at his sole expense for about three years, at 300 Rupees per month. The condition ■■ which Dr. Buchanan engaged to maintain him ■■ the Mission House, was, That one of the elder Missionaries, and three at least of the

12. If your Lordship should judge it expedient to investigate any of the facts contained in this letter, I shall be happy to afford any further evidence or explanation that may be required, before I leave India.

I have the honour to be,

My Lord,

With the highest respect, your Lordship's

Most obedient and humble Servant,

(Signed) C. BUCHANAN.

Calcutta,
7th Nov. 1807.

---

youths, should engage in the diligent study of the Chinese Language. Mr. Marshman was the elder Missionary who accepted the condition. Hearing that the Hon. the Court of Directors were about to organize the College at Hertford, Dr. Buchanan contemplated, at that time, the probability of Mr. Lassar's pupils being by and by qualified to hold a situation as instructors of Chinese in that institution. They are now qualified for that office; and it seems to be the interest of the East India Company to appropriate the special advantage. A knowledge of the Chinese Language is confessed to be of the utmost importance to their civil servants who have to negociate with the Chinese people; and yet it is not cultivated either at the College of Fort William in Bengal, or at the College of Hertford in England. This important language, hitherto deemed inaccessible to the Universities of Europe, was planted, and has been brought to maturity, as it were, by the way side.

Alexander Duff

India, and India Missions. Edinburgh: J. Johnstone, 1839.

CHAPTER IV.

THE GOSPEL, THE ONLY EFFECTUAL INSTRUMENT IN REGENERATING INDIA—GENERAL CONSIDERATION OF THE AGENCY TO BE EMPLOYED IN ITS PROPAGATION.

Various expedients proposed for remedying the evils under which India has for ages groaned—Some of these briefly reviewed —The Scheme of Political Reform—The Scheme of Economic Reform—The Scheme of Secular Education Reform—The Scheme of Temporizing Religious Reform—All these nugatory—The Gospel, the only effectual instrument of genuine Reformation—Illustration of this—The practical question proposed, How, or by what means is the Gospel to be most successfully propagated?—Quotation from the Author of the Natural History of Enthusiasm—The three generic measures, Christian Education of the Young, Preaching to the Adults, and the Circulation of the Bible—These not antagonists, but mutual friends and allies—In reference to Education, the practical question considered, Whether is it better at the outset, to pursue the direct method of attempting at once to impart a general elementary knowledge to the many, or the indirect method of attempting to reach the many through the instrumentality of the instructed few?—In reference to Preaching, the great practical question considered, Who ought to be the preachers?—General reasons adduced, to prove that they ought to be natives—The inadequate supply of existing missionary stations—Prodigious disproportion between the number of labourers and the extent of the field—Occasional itineracy, a very inefficient means of evangelization—Different causes of this pointed out—Superiority of the localizing system—Other arguments, besides the numerical one, in favour of an extensive native agency—The diminution of expense—The necessity of the mode of life being such as to bring a holy example fully to bear upon the people—The necessity of a familiar acquaintance with the tones and idiom of speech; the manners, habits, and prevalent modes of thinking—Natives, the real reformers of their own country—How qualified natives are to be raised—Objections to Education Institutions in connection with the missionary enterprise considered—That missionaries are thereby converted into Teachers, Professors, and Lecturers, instead of being Preachers—That the scheme is different from that which was blessed with a Pentacostal effusion—That it is contrary to Apostolic example—This allegation examined at length in its various bearings—Circulation of the Bible—Question considered as to the amount of good to be expected from the written word in the absence of the living voice to direct attention towards it—To raise up a native agency ought to be not a secondary, but a primary object, in conducting the missionary enterprise—Happy day for India, when through the instrumentality of the educational and other means employed, qualified natives shall become the Christian teachers, preachers, and translators to their countrymen !

SUPPOSE the vital pulse of a nation to be for ages animated, its internal spring and life for ages saturated and leavened with the spirit of such a system as that of Hinduism,—a system which, by confounding the creature with the Creator, tends to annihilate the very feeling of moral responsibility, or, if conscience will speak out, points to a scheme by which man may practically assume to himself the merit of all that is good, and attribute to Deity the demerit of all that is evil :—Suppose the external form and manifestation of a nation's life to be for ages cast into the mould of those countless observances which are the spontaneous growth and product of such a system as that of Hinduism,—observances beneath the shelter of whose divine sanction or divinely appointed expiations there is no act of lying or deceit, fraud or dishonesty, vice or immorality, theft or plunder, devastation or bloodshed, which may not be perpetrated with a free and fearless impunity as to future retribution :—Suppose a nation to be for ages so inwardly saturated, and so outwardly moulded, what could we expect to find as the resulting condition of the myriads of its people?—What could we possibly expect, unless a condition the most degraded and demoralized, the most wretched and miserable? And is not this, by universal consent, the present condition of the millions of India?

Suppose, next, salvation and eternity were for the moment kept out of view;—suppose our consideration were wholly limited to the narrow span of time, and it were simply asked, How is the temporal estate of India's teeming population to be ameliorated,—their personal, domestic, and social happiness to be augmented,—their individual and national character to be elevated and improved? What must be the soundest and most enlightened reply?

In the endeavour to return a practical response to such a question, the men of this world are not slow in propounding their varied specifics. Those who attribute most of the evils to the influence of a grinding despotism tell us, that the establishment of a representative government and free institutions—the investiture of the great body of the people with municipal rights and political privileges—would, by achieving their emancipation from a tyrannical yoke, raise them in the scale of civilization, comfort, and earthly felicity. What enlightened mind is not ready to acknowledge such a government and institutions, such rights and privileges, to be among the greatest of temporal blessings—and productive of the greatest temporal good? But does not all experience prove that these must be the *effects*,—the *results* of something *antecedent*,—ere they can become the *causes* of any real and lasting *consequent* good?—For what are the institutions and privileges in question?—What, but the visible forms in which certain previously excogitated opinions and cherished principles are embodied?—What, but the external organs for the full manifestation and developement of these principles and opinions? To attempt, therefore, to regenerate a people by bestowing upon them free institutions at the very outset,—when as yet they are literally steeped in the very slough of bondage intellectual moral and religious, individual social and political,—is surely to *begin at the wrong end*. It is to confer forms that are the sensible vehicles of principles and opinions totally alien from those which ages have rendered inveterate! It is to bestow physical organs adapted and designed to manifest principles and opinions absolutely diverse from those which immemorial usage has tended to consecrate. What is this but to attempt to convey to an infant the strength of a giant, by forcing into its hands the club of Hercules?—or to impart to a fool the wisdom of a philosopher, by investing him with an Academician's gown?—or to convert an Icelandic waste into a tropical garden, by suddenly transplanting into it the saplings of palmiras and tamarinds? Incongruous and abortive attempts! *First*, convey to the infant the giant's strength,—and the new-born vigour will spontaneously exhibit itself in seeking for the giant's weapons. Impart to the fool the intellectual energy of the philosopher,—and this rare endowment will spontaneously develope itself through the medium of appropriate external symbols. Communicate to the sterile waste the heat and moisture of a tropical clime,—and these vivifying powers will spontaneously manifest themselves in the most luxuriant produce. In like manner, *first* imbue the mind of an enslaved people with the true spirit, the true genius, the true sentiment of rational freedom,—and these will speedily manifest their inherent power by shaking off, like old fashioned and worn out garments, the positive forms and organs of an oppressive despotism; and, at one and the same time, clothing themselves in the representative forms, and developing themselves through the congenial organs of a free constitution,—with its equitable sanctions, rights, privileges, and laws.

Others,—convinced of the impossibility of effecting, and the consequent mockery of pretending to effect, the regeneration of an utterly ignorant and depraved populace by any merely political expedients,—have recourse to the plans and projects of the Economists. The impoverished and famished condition of the people, say they, is the originating cause of most of their miseries. Only increase their wealth, their capital, or the means of personal comfort and refinement,—

and you will render them happy and flourishing. In order to this, there must be a diminution of the land-tax and other public burdens;—there must be the introduction of an enlightened system of commerce;—there must be a skilful developement of the internal resources of the country;—there must be the application of machinery to the varied products of a soil exhaustless in its fertility;—there must be increased facilities for communication and exchange by the construction of roads and railways, canals and bridges. Now, all this is very good, excellent, and praiseworthy, so far as it goes. What philanthropist would not rejoice to promote any plan which promised to effect the alleviation of human suffering—the augmentation of human bliss? But, in the present circumstances of India, is not such a scheme of economical reform, equally with that of political reform,—when proposed as the *primary antecedent* measure,—obnoxious to the grand objection of *beginning at the end instead of the beginning?* Or, even if it were not, how would its most unbounded success secure the great ultimate end in view, viz., the real prosperity and permanent happiness of the people? Suppose the wealth of every individual,—from the humble occupant of a bambu hut, to the lordly proprietor of a marble palace—were increased tenfold, or a hundredfold, what influence, immediate and controlling, would mere affluence exert in bridling passion, extirpating vice, demolishing superstition? Rather, while the mind and morals of the people remained unreclaimed, would not the inevitable tendency of an increase of wealth be, to open up an enlarged sphere for the indulgence of every wayward desire and propensity of corrupt nature? While the spirit of Hinduism remained in its entireness, would not an ampler scope be afforded for the manifestation of its baneful power? The enhanced profits of the lower orders, instead of being transferred to the public treasury, would go to swell their offerings to priests and idols. The larger revenues of the noble and the powerful, instead of being applied to develope the boundless capabilities of the soil, would be expended in throwing new splendour over the celebration of rites and festivals;

which might minister to their pride and love of fame in this life, and hold out the prospect of raising them to the enjoyments of a higher heaven in the next. The improved resources of the Brahmans, instead of being appropriated to real enlightenment of the popular mind, would be lavished in restoring and multiplying those purely scholastic seminaries and idolatrous fanes and other establishments,—so well calculated to command the reverence, to rivet the mind and heart, to engross the passions and interests, and to enstamp the manners and customs of a sensuous apathetic imaginative people. The improved facilities of intercommunion between the different provinces would only tend greatly to augment the number, and prolong the period, of meritorious pilgrimages to distant shrines and other holy places. In this way, every additional increment to mere wealth, instead of insuring a harvest of reformation and enduring prosperity, might only enlarge the springheads of that general corruption which must ever terminate in confusion and ruin. Chains of iron might, for a while, be converted into chains of gold, but the people would be manacled and miserable still;—and only the more hopelessly miserable, inasmuch as the road to destruction would be strewn with more alluring, though not less illusive fascinations.

Persuaded that if men be vicious and depraved, mere wealth would either leave them unchanged for the better, or make them more vicious and depraved than before, numbers have risen up to assert that something more is indispensable. Ignorance say they, ignorance of the laws of nature and of all true science is the main source of vice and unhappiness. Only give men knowledge,—useful scientific knowledge,—and you will enlighten, reclaim, and elevate them to a new platform of earthly bliss. As if the wisdom of this world were resolved as long as possible to pass bye the only efficacious instrument, morals and religion have been excluded from this reforming scheme! And since both in India and in Britain it has found the ablest advocates, it is well to consider its peculiar adaptation to the end in view.

How often have we heard of the streams of " useful knowledge" flowing through the land, and fertilizing the intellects of the people into a rich harvest of reason and intelligence. Yea, after the manner and amplitude of Oriental hyperbole, how often have we heard this knowledge compared to a mighty ocean which has already begun, and is finally destined to encompass the whole world of intellectual being? Well, granting for a moment to the adorers of knowledge their very heart's desire, might we not, for their special edification, push their own parallel into a few particulars? Modern knowledge, say they, is like the great ocean, seen to roll its waters on every shore! What then?—and if, like the great ocean, it has its serviceable tides, may it not have its destructive inundations too? If, like the great ocean, it has its depths profound, may it not have its straits and shallows too? If, like the great ocean, it has its roads and havens, may it not have its rocks and quicksands too? If, like the great ocean, it has its gales and gentle breezes, may it not have its storms and tempests too?

But are we left to *mere hypotheses* on this subject? No. Let us then briefly advert to the mode in which *human knowledge without religion* does, in point of fact, usually operate. Experience amply testifies that every where the heart of man is naturally proud and selfish; his intellect dark and degraded. And while selfishness leads him to convert his own progress in any branch of knowledge into a test of its superior excellence, the degradation of his intellect slavishly binds him to the exclusive pursuit of that which is *merely natural;* having no spontaneous relish for those sublimer spiritual truths, that specially concern the interests of eternity. This knowledge, however, from its variety, seizes, and from its adaptation to the natural intellect, fills all the avenues of the soul. Hence, the man who is much occupied with his favourite theme, soon becoming enamoured of it, gradually attains to proficiency; and, at last, succeeds in acquiring a reputation for learning and wisdom. This, very naturally, redoubles his zeal and his diligence. As he proceeds, his intellect grows in strength; and becomes rampant with confidence. It exults in detecting the weaknesses and failures of others; it glories in its own acquirements and achievements; it trusts implicitly to its own sagacity, and relies exclusively on its own resources; it is filled with self-sufficiency, and swoln with self-conceit;—and, as the very frequency with which it may have formed theories and pictures of morality and religion, too often renders it insensible to the practical obligations of both, it soon acknowledges no master,—pronounces its own light to be sufficient, —scorning to yield reverence even to the High and Holy One; who alone is Light, and Truth, and Life, and Goodness. Every unsanctified intellect thus becomes a tyrant; every master intellect a master tyrant. The more splendid the talents, the deeper the shades that are cast on a nature already, alas, very dark, and very depraved! The more towering the genius, the more tremendous the engine, for spreading devastation through the empire of truth and order, godliness and sobriety!

Now, when many are so trained, so disciplined, and so prepared, society,—like the luxuriant, but deceitful verdure that clothes the precincts of the volcano—has attained to its state of greatest external brilliancy and internal decay:—and the elements that long slumbered, only to accumulate the greater strength, must at length burst forth in desolating fury. All bonds are broken; all obligations dissolved; all rights abolished; all government subverted; and all things sacred and profane trampled under foot by a tyranny that is merciless, just in proportion to the light, and knowledge, and power of the unsanctified intellect.

Is this an imaginary picture? Would to God that it were! Unless all history be a riddle, and its lessons the visions of a dreamer, this in the present corrupt state of human nature, is a portraiture of the inevitable *tendency* of all unsanctified knowledge—a tendency, to which the experience of ages bears its unimpeachable testimony. But why refer to past ages? Why not to the events of our own day ?—and amongst these, why not to the most terrible exemplification of the ***tendency and effects of knowledge without religion***, recorded in the annals of all time ! Some of the original founders of the modern French philosophy, about the middle of last century, were, beyond all debate, in their own sense of the term, philanthropists. For, was not theirs a system, which, without the aid of religion at all, according to their own calculation, was to regenerate the world ? Before their system, was not barbarism every where to give place to civilization—preponderant rights to equality—and tyranny to liberty ? Was not truth, so long buried beneath the rubbish of centuries of ignorance and error, to experience a species of resurrection ? Was not reason, so long befooled by prejudice and superstition, to be restored to her rightful ascendancy in the intellectual firmament ? In a word, was not the new philosophy to construct an altar whence the flames were expected to ascend and spread and brighten, till they poured the stream of illumination round the globe ?

Magnificent rising sun of promise !—doomed how ingloriously to set in darkness ? Alas ! the heart of man is deceitful above all things, and desperately wicked ; who can know it ? Not one who does not see it clearly reflected in the spotless mirror of God's own word. The Encyclopædists and Economists, and the whole body of fraternizing Illuminati of France, in casting that eternal word in derision away from them, did thereby cast away the only lamp that would have guided them through the labyrinth of the heart's natural perverseness. Who then need wonder that, wholly ignorant as they were of the real nature of the disease, they should have blundered fatally in prescribing a remedy ? And has not the disastrous issue accordingly shown that, instead of kindling a light which might illuminate the world, they were only fanning a flame that was soon to envelope it in a general conflagration ?

Ah ! if one of the better-intentioned of the earlier fathers of the new philosophy had only arisen from the grave ; and alighted in the vale of Paris during the midnight gloom of the Reign of Terror ;—if, there, he had met, in personified forms, his own Philosophy metamorphosed into undisguised Atheism, openly proclaiming that there was no God, and that death was an eternal sleep ;—and, along with Atheism, her legitimate offspring, savage Anarchy, wielding his tremendous scimitar ; fresh reeking with the blood of thousands of unhappy victims, slaughtered in the name of humanity.—Ah ! methinks, he would start back as aghast at the hideous aspect of his own double progeny, as the "Archangel fallen," from the shapeless monsters he encountered at the gates of Pandemonium ! And, like the thunder-stricken Seraph, he might thus break silence :—

"Whence and what art thou, execrable shape,
That dar'st, though grim and terrible, advance
Thy miscreated front athwart my way ?
* * * * *
What thing thou art thus double formed ? and why,
In this infernal vale first met, thou call'dst
Me Father, and that phantom call'dst my Son ?
I know thee not, and never saw till now
Sight more detestable than him and thee."

To whom his own darling Philosophy, now transformed into naked, hideous Atheism, might thus reply :—

"Hast thou forgot me, then, and do I seem
Now in thine eye so foul ? once deem'd so fair.
* * * when at th' Assembly * * * *
* * * * * * with thee combin'd
In bold conspiracy againt heaven's King,
Likest to thee in shape and countenance bright,
Then shining heav'nly fair, a goddess arm'd,
Out of thy head I sprung."

Instantly demon Anarchy, Atheism's natural child, stands forth,—

"Fierce as ten furies, terrible as hell."

With earthquake shock he falls upon the hapless father.—More successful in the onslaught than his Pandemonian prototype, he drags him quivering to the guillotine—and speedily holds up his severed head to the gaze of a frenzied multitude ;—an everlasting monument of the triumph of philosophy without religion—of the golden age of equal rights—of the halcyon reign of unbounded liberty!

After an example so recent and so calamitous, would it not indicate something like insanity to attempt to regenerate a country like India, by means of human philosophy and human science alone? Hinduism,—which is so huge a compound of all that is false monstrous and extravagant in every department of knowledge, physical literary and religious,—could not long resist the vigorous onset of European science, if conducted on a scale of *national* magnitude. In the sudden demolition of established systems and established forms,—and in the entire absence of *positive principles* of counteractive power,—the newly awakened spirit might spring at one bound into the opposite extreme;—manifesting itself in actions and events, from the dim and distant contemplation of which, even in imagination, the mind most gladly retires. Exhausted at length by its own convulsive efforts, the sceptical and irreligious spirit might become stripped of all vital energy; while, as in the case of other revolutions, its very excesses of incredulity and indiscriminate outrage might produce a powerful reaction in favour of the ancient creed. The national mind of a people like that of India—among whom the religious sentiment or propensity has ever been manifested with peculiar power,—might, with greater fervour than ever, rally round the standards of a faith which, though fiercely proscribed, had still lingered and survived behind the entrenchment of customs manners and usages, rendered inveterate by the practice of ages;—and might, with greater tenacity than ever, cling to forms and observances, the abrogation of which had entailed nought but devastation and ruin; and the absence of which had left a vacuum not to be supplied by the dim abstractions of science or the frigid speculations of philosophy. In a word, the temples might be repaired; the idols reseated; the offerings and sacrifices renewed; the rites and ceremonies reinstituted; and the festivals celebrated with greater pomp and magnificence than ever. In either case, whether viewed in its direct operation, simply as the destroyer (without supplying a substitute),—or in its reaction, as the restorer of a system like that of Hinduism, what becomes of the boasted power of mere human science to raise a people circumstanced as are the Hindus to the enjoyment of a sort of millenium of temporal bliss? Alas, alas, from first to last—from beginning to end,—it is all mockery and delusion, as pregnant with disaster as with disappointment and shame!

Constrained by the united voice of reason and experience, many of the leaders of public opinion on such subjects as the present, have at length confessed that no where is ignorant vicious enslaved man to be regenerated by mere political, economic, or philosophic reforms. They do now profess to tell us, in no faint whispers, that morals and religion of some description are absolutely necessary for the organization and maintenance of a free and happy state of society. This is a truth which almost all in every age, who have sounded the depths of the human spirit in its varied wants cravings and appetencies, have been constrained to proclaim. The acknowledgment of it is a concession which has often been extorted from the practical penetrative sagacity of men, who, in their own lives, gave fatal evidence that they would falsify it if they could. "That religion," remarks Lord Bolingbroke, "is necessary to strengthen, and that it contributes to the support of government, cannot be denied without contradicting reason and experience both." Again, "to make government effectual to all the good purposes of it, there *must be* a religion; this religion must be national, and this national religion must be maintained in reputation and reverence." The iron-hearted Robespierre, in that ever-memorable conclave which voted that there was no God, could boldly protest against the political inexpediency of the decision; exclaiming, "If there were no God; a wise government would invent one!" Napoleon, according to the authority of a modern French Statesman, was heard on one occasion to declare:—"No society can exist without morals; and there can be no sound morals without religion. Hence, there is no firm or durable bulwark for a State, but what religion constructs; let, therefore, every school throughout the land, assume the precepts of religion as the basis of instruction. Experience has torn the veil from our eyes." And of late it has become *almost the fashion*, even in some of our great secular assemblies, from the Senate downwards, to moralize in a somewhat similar strain.

But though the necessity of morals and religion of some kind be now so openly and generally acknowledged, there is the same perverse infatuation as ever in obstinately rejecting the only genuine morality, the only true religion;—and that is, the Christianity of the Bible, the soul-awakening soul-purifying Gospel of our Lord and Saviour Jesus Christ. To this, however, *it must come in the end*. When human intellect has put forth all its strength and failed; when human ingenuity has exhausted all its devices in vain; when human reason has stood on the terminating point of the last promontory of that shore which bounds its dominion, and has gazed at the outermost horizon which circumscribes the range of its expedients, without discovering the object of pursuit:—then will the spirit of universal man be driven in despair, if not allured by persuasion, to recoil back upon the only real specific,—the only infallible panacea which has been provided by God Himself. To talk, as many in high places are at present disposed to do,—to talk of resorting to a species of *syncretism* or *eclecticism* in religion, somewhat similar to that which characterised the struggles of an expiring Paganism, that would open a pantheon for the amicable cohabitation of the gods of all nations,—somewhat similar to that which characterised the death-throes of heathen Philosophy, that would amalgamate the peculiar opinions of the founders of all religions, and educe therefrom some depurated ultimate doctrine virtually comprehensive of them all:—to talk any longer of resorting to some such scheme as would thus toss the articles and confessions, the liturgies and homilies of all religionists, however heterogeneous, into one intellectual cauldron; so that out of the fermentation consequent on the commingling of such discordant materials, there might bring forth some volatilized substance which may be pronounced the common essence of them all ;—and then to propose rearing schools and temples wherein this etherialized decoction may be worshipped as a common idol by the countless throng of votaries, between the extremes of massive Apostolic Christianity and the unsubstantial shadow of leanest lankest Deism :—seriously to talk, in this epoch of the world's history, of any such scheme being practicable, is an outrage to all experience,—to talk of it as desirable, if practicable, an insult to common sense, —to talk of it as an optimism, even if practicable, and to the carnal mind desirable, a daring affront to the Majesty of the Most High !

Seeing then that all ameliorating schemes of mere human devising must in the issue prove abortive,—that even if success should attend them up to their full measure of capacity for effecting good, they must still prove but poor, weak, and insufficient measures, which—

> " Will but skin and film the ulcerous part,
> While rank corruption mining all within,
> Infects unseen,"—

what remains, but that we should at once betake ourselves to that only effective scheme which is announced and developed in the blessed Volume of Inspiration ? And though that scheme has *primarily* in view not the physical health and well-being of the body, but the spiritual health and salvation of the soul,—not the petty concerns of time, but the momentous interests of eternity,—the slightest consideration will suffice to show how the less is necessarily involved in the greater ; how an adequate provision for realizing the felicities of heaven is the best and surest guarantee for enjoying the noblest heritage of happiness on earth.

In order to be fully assured of this, let us simply ask, What is the *central point* around which the whole scheme of Hinduism in its theory and practice is made to turn ? It is,—that sinful man by his own sufficiency, his own services, his own works, his own meritorious obedience, can propitiate God, and earn to himself a right and title to immortal bliss. If man really knew God in His holiness; and God's law as the perfect transcript of that holiness, he would be overwhelmed with the conviction of his utter inability to propitiate his offended Maker, or fulfil the whole of His law. Hence, would he be filled with hatred and enmity against that law which must denounce, and that God who must punish, all transgression. Hence, too,—as he could not altogether shake off the impression of the being and providence of God; or of the obligation of obeying His holy law,—he would in time be tempted and impelled to feign a deity like unto himself, and a divine law suited to his own impaired capacity of obedience;—a deity whom he could appease if he willed;—a law which he could fulfil if it suited his good pleasure. Hence, accordingly, the fundamental cause, source, and origin of Hinduism; and of every other scheme of false religion. The system of Hinduism is nothing else than a stupendous superstructure raised upon this one grand central principle as its foundation-stone—namely, the principle of *exclusive self-reliance*, *exclusive self-righteousness*,—a self-righteousness far more absolute than that of Roman Catholicism itself, which would combine and harmonize grace and desert, faith and good works. Hence, the countless round of daily and almost hourly rites, ceremonies, and observances,—the countless round of fastings, pilgrimages, and rehearsals of holy texts,—the countless round of gifts, offerings, and sacrifices,—the countless round of ablutions, expiations, and atonements,—the countless round of austerities, self-inflicted tortures, and religious suicides,—the countless round of inquiries into the nature of things, meditations, and absorbed contemplations;—all, all circulate for ever around the grand central, but false and detestable, principle that man, though fallen and sinful, may work out by his own unaided strength a title to the divine favour, a right to celestial rewards or to supreme beatitude. The colossal scheme of Hinduism, as has already been shown, does embrace, and intimately incorporate with itself, all imaginable departments of Tradition, Literature, Science and Art,—but these are like so many columns, capitals, and minarets, designed to garnish the inner citadel of self-righteousness; or so many walls, towers, and buttresses, intended to render it more firm, secure and unassailable.

This being the foundation-stone of the immense fabric of Hinduism, let us now see with what divine precision Christianity is adapted to wrench it from its position; overturn the superimposed edifice; and drive the ploughshare of destruction over the crumbling ruins. For what in the mighty system of Revelation, is that central truth around which all other truths revolve? It is,—that not by any exertions, endeavours, works, or sufferings of our own, can we ever be justified before God; but solely through "the righteousness of God," revealed from heaven,—the righteousness which God Himself hath effected and provided,—the real, true, and everlasting righteousness, or perfect obedience to the divine law both in its threatened penalties and inflexible requirements, which was exemplified by Christ, our Immanuel; —a righteousness which is freely and gratuitously, out of undeserved love and mere mercy imputed to us; and—without money or price, doing or suffering, service or merit of any kind—received by faith alone;—a righteousness which, when so imputed and received, is as really made over to us, as if we ourselves had wrought it out by a perfect fulfilment of the law in all its penalties and threatenings, as well as precepts and commands—as really accounted to be our own as if we ourselves had endured the infinite and eternal punishment due to our transgressions; and at the same time had magnified the law and made it honourable by a perfect conformity to all its demands, whether in the way of duties to be performed, or of prohibitions to be inviolably respected. The moment this perfect righteousness is,—through the instrumentality of that faith which is itself the gift of God,—imputed to the believer, he is pardoned and justified from all sin; freed from the sentence of condemnation; acquitted of the guilt of transgression; and entitled to "an inheritance which is incorruptible, and undefiled, and that fadeth not away, reserved in heaven." No wonder that the bringing in of this finished, this spotless righteousness, should be extolled as the chief even of Jehovah's works,—the clear manifestation thereof, as the crowning excellency of Revelation,—the universal proclamation thereof, as "the Gospel of the Gospel,"—and the free imputation thereof to hell-deserving rebels, as the very consummation of Infinite Wisdom, Holiness, and Love!

What a revolution would the effectual lodgmēnt of this single primal truth—"that we are made righteous before God, and continue so, by grace alone; through the mere imputation of the righteousness or meritorious obedience and sufferings of Christ; the only perfect righteousness which can be maintained against wrath, sin, death, and hell,"—achieve in the national mind of a people so impregnated with the spirit of self-righteousness as the native inhabitants of India! And blessed be God, that in attempting to secure an effectual lodgment of it in the understandings and hearts of men, we are not left to mere human instruction, to mere human persuasion. No; we have the promise of the presence of the Divine Redeemer Himself, and of the efficacious influence of His Almighty Spirit. Behold, then, how the believing and influential embracement of this one vital and fundamental doctrine would hurl away the entire mass of morbid fears, and legal sentiments, and meritorious observances, which, in the course of ages, have grown up into a gigantic system, crushing and paralyzing the souls and bodies of myriads of myriads! Let the great body of the people be once brought—through the word of truth, sent home by the energy of the Holy Spirit—to sing aloud with Luther, "Thou Lord Jesus art my righteousness, but I am thy sin; Thou hast taken to thee what was mine, and hast given to me what was thine; Thou hast taken upon thee what thou wast not, and given to me what I was not,"—and how must the all-comprehending system of Hinduism evanish! An absolute confidence in one almighty, omniscient, omnipresent Mediator and Advocate, would at once supersede the necessity of applying to any one of the legions of secondary mediators whether on earth or in heaven.—Hence would the power and tyranny of the Brahmanical and celestial hierarchies be for ever broken; and the constantly recurring demand for gifts and invocations to secure their favour and intercession be for ever removed. An absolute belief that an almighty and all-merciful Redeemer hath actually fulfilled to the uttermost all the righteous ordinances of an immutable law, in the stead of sinners,—and that he is both able and willing to impute to them, on believing, his own all-perfect obedience or active righteousness,—would at once expose the futility of their own poor, lame, inadequate self-justifying performances.—Hence would follow a clear perception and operative conviction of the worse than uselessness of the attempts to restore peace and comfort in a troubled, pained, and restless conscience, or to earn a heavenly recompense, by resorting to the endless rites, forms, and ceremonies,—with all the half-gorgeous, half-barbaric pomps and vanities of Brahmanical worship,—and the whole vast apparatus of works and services of minor, secondary, or transcendent merit. For who, to adopt, once more, one of Luther's pointed expressions, "Who, that could soar with eagle's wings to the Sun of Righteousness itself, would not be rejoiced to throw his crutches away?" An absolute assurance that an almighty Saviour hath actually offered himself, in the stead of sinners, as a complete oblation and satisfaction to divine justice—and that he has thereby drained off the full cup of merited retribution, and exhausted the full measure of threatened vengeance,—must lay bare the utter nugatoriness of the endeavour to supplant or supplement, in whole or in part, an all-perfect and freely imputed passive righteousness, by any voluntary sufferings of their own.—Hence, at once would be swept away the boundless variety of self-inflicted austerities, penances, and mortifications, which are intended to diminish and gradually to exhaust the amount of penalties incurred by transgression; as well as the entire host of expedients designed to effect a deliverance from the purgatorial processes of transmigration in this world, and of penal severities in the regions below.

In this way would the Gospel of salvation at a single stroke,—by its one grand essential doctrine of justification through faith alone in the meritorious obedience and sufferings or all-sufficient all-prevailing righteousness of Immanuel,—"God manifest in the flesh,"—smite the stupendous fabric of Hinduism, and grind it to powder;—and, over its scattered dust erect a temple, the foundation of which would be the Rock of Ages; and every stone of which would be a living stone, glistening in the radiance of celestial truth, and tuneful with the hosannahs of seraphic melody. How different the Divine from every human instrument of reformation! How wise, how gracious, how mighty the scheme of Divine appointment compared with the weak, partial, inadequate, temporizing expedients and devices of man! The former does not, like the latter, confine itself to mere externals and outworks. It is not satisfied with the attempt to rectify one or other of the more objectionable observances of worship,—to controvert one or other of the more absurd and pernicious abstract principles,—to uproot one or other of the more cruel and abominable usages,—to lop off one or other of the more monstrous excrescences in the forms and institutions of general polity,—to expose one or other of the more palpable disfigurations of truth by scholastic and metaphysical subtilties,—to reinvigorate one or other of the more debilitated of the intellectual faculties. No: its grand aim and design is, to penetrate at once beneath the surface, and strike a deadly blow at the root of the whole mischief. And having extirpated the self-justifying pride, the inbred self-righteousness,—which spontaneously springs up in the soil of every human heart,—by the introduction and substitution of a spotless, because Divine righteousness, it sweeps away the very foundation of the palladium of all error in theory, and of all ungodliness in practice.

When once sinful guilty man has been led thus to renounce his own righteousness, with all its "filthy rags" and shackles and bondages of "dead works,"—and has been made to stand erect, because accounted guiltless, in the righteousness of Christ,—he begins to breathe the air, and to act under the inspiration of that liberty wherewith the truth has made him free. And being made free,—free from the accusations of conscience, the claims of violated justice, the condemnations of an outraged law,—free from the fear of subordinate agencies, celestial, terrestrial, or infernal,—free from the terrors of death, and the grave, and everlasting perdition,—he is filled, he cannot but be filled, with solid peace and consolation, joy and gladness;—he is animated, he cannot but be animated, with a cheerful boldness, an undaunted courage, a holy intrepidity;—he pours forth, he cannot but pour forth, the song of triumph,—"If God be for us, who can be against us? It is God that justifieth, who is he that condemneth? He that spared not His own Son, but delivered Him up for us all, how shall He not with Him also freely give us all things?"

Now, when man is thus delivered,—not merely from all the external constraints of a never-ending round of burdensome ordinances, but from all the internal constraints of an ever-present burden of guilt and fear,—a glow of joyous generous warmth is diffused over the whole soul, fresh and reviving like the radiant blush of morn. It then prepares to start, as it were, by a free and elastic spring, into hitherto untrodden paths; and plumes its wings for a sustained flight into hitherto unvisited regions. No longer pressed down at every turn by the incubus of artificial mechanical prescriptions, the mind uncoils itself from the incrustation of ages; begins to develope its dormant activities; and shoots out its emancipated energies, with happiest effect, in every direction. Then will the spirit of inquiry penetrate every department of human research.—The mutual rights of governors and governed; the reciprocal bonds of priests and people; the rise and progress of society; the foundations of every system of knowledge, human or divine; the design, fitness, and adaptation of all existing forms and schemes of polity, civil or sacred;—all, all will be fearlessly investigated. Then will the genius of true liberty, no longer chained down by the fetters of despotism, spontaneously embody itself in free institutions. Then will the genius of a wise economy, no longer bound to lavish its affluence in ministering to the "pomp and circumstance" of a lordly hierarchy of priests and idols, spontaneously expend its accumulated stores in multiplying the sources of human comfort and enjoyment. Then too, will the genius of literature, science, and art, no longer foreclosed by finding every field preoccupied with the erroneous dogmata of an infallible authority, spontaneously roam at large over the wide domain of time and space, matter and spirit. New worlds will be disclosed to view, and fresh illumination shed upon the old. And thus will Christianity, by being primarily the great Evangelizer, vindicate unto itself the inalienable prerogative of being secondarily the only effectual Liberator, Intellectualizer, Civilizer and Comforter of man!

Ought we then, in the first instance, to discourage or discountenance any direct attempts to better the temporal condition of the people of India, by repairing their municipal and other civil institutions, drawing forth the natural resources of their soil, or increasing the amount of their general intelligence? With solemnity of feeling we would reply, God forbid! Let any and every effort of this description be put forth, which the benevolence of man can devise, or the state of native society can admit. Such endeavours may be prosecuted *cotemporaneously* with the evangelizing process. All of these may be made to advance *pari passu*; though the latter is beyond all measure the most potent in its operation, and the most extensive in its results. And, in very proportion as it succeeds, will the former be grafted upon the native stock, naturalized, and made to bear independent fruits. All that we demand and insist on is, that that scheme should be held as supreme, to which alone the palm of supremacy is due,—that that engine should be chiefly wielded and placed in forefront of the battle, which alone can win for us a decisive victory. And we now do, and must for ever strenuously contend, that whoever sincerely and honestly desires to see India emancipated, prosperous and flourishing as regards the things of time, does cast away from him the only instrument which can effectually realize the very flower and fruit of his own wishes, when, in blind fatuity, he nauseates and spurns the blessed Gospel with its unsearchable riches of free grace. Greatly, however, as we ought to rejoice at the vast retinue of temporal amelioration which must ever follow in the train of a conquering Gospel; yet ought we most chiefly to rejoice at the more glorious retinue of spiritual blessings which constitute the very consummation of its triumphs. To see human beings,—once sunk in wretchedness and barbarism, whether arrayed in tattered rags or gilded with tinsel splendour,—now encompassed with a rich profusion of the comforts and enjoyments of civilized life,—to see them exhibit in their conduct all the courtesies, decencies, and tender humanities of refined society,—is, no doubt, a lovely and cheering spectacle. But to see human beings,—at one time the slaves of sin, the bondsmen of Satan, and the heirs of perdition,—now freed from the guilt and power of sin, delivered from the tyranny of Satan, and reinstalled as heirs of glory, honour, and immortality,—is surely a spectacle transcendently more beauteous and exhilarating. And were both spectacles combined in one, where should we find language to pourtray the excellencies of so glorious a combination? But both have been, and may be conjoined in harmonious union. And the mighty power which can unite and realize them both, is that very Gospel which, though weakness and foolishness in the eyes of men, is in the hands of an Almighty Spirit, " the power of God and the wisdom of God unto salvation." So that to the blessed Gospel belongs in the loftiest and most sublime sense, the incommunicable privilege of having " the promise of the life that now is, as well as of that which is to come." Accordingly when,—in direct contradiction to all the schemes and projects of all the politicians, economists, intellectual educationists, and liberalizing religionists in the world,—we boldly aver, that the only real, the only adequate, the only infallible remedy for the numberless evils connected with time and eternity, under which India and other heathen lands have for ages groaned, is the glorious Gospel of our Lord and Saviour Jesus Christ, we at once entrench ourselves in an impregnable fortress,—a fortress which has the unchangeableness of the divine decrees for its foundation; and the covenanted security of all the divine attributes for its bulwarks of defence.

In this momentous conclusion, all of every denomination, who love the Lord Jesus in sincerity and in truth, must joyously acquiesce. The only question which can arise amongst them, or which can possibly occasion any difference of opinion is the great practical one, How, or in what way, or by what means can we most effectually communicate the saving knowledge of Jesus Christ, and Him crucified? On this important subject, it affords us unfeigned pleasure to be enabled to introduce a passage from the pen of one of the most powerful and original of the religious writers of the present day,—a passage which expresses sentiments the *very same in substance* with those which we have been reiterating, both in India and in Britain, for years before we met with the work which contains it. "The obligation," remarks the author of the History of Natural Enthusiasm, "the obligation we are under, of attempting to convert our erring brethren to the faith of Christ, is not more clear than is the principle under the guidance of which we are to proceed in discharging the part assigned to us. Christian teachers wield no supernatural arms; they are simply—*teachers:* the utmost they can do is to instruct and to persuade; and in the accomplishment of their task, they are bound to avail themselves of all those methods of influence which experience authenticates, and which Christianity does not condemn. It is true that the conversion of men is a divine work; but it is not the less the work of human zeal, industry, and discretion; and we are just as fully bound to use our utmost sagacity in the discharge of our part, as to discharge it at all.

"It is certainly very proper to keep in view the abstract idea of preaching the Gospel, and to think of it simply as an announcement of pardon to those who, like ourselves, are guilty and condemned, and yet are heirs of immortality. In this general view the sons of Adam, of every tribe, stand, without distinction, on the same ground; and in this view nothing more seems to be included in the idea of a mission to the heathen, than the sending forth of men who, having themselves become partakers of the grace of God, glow with holy zeal and love towards their brethren, and are willing to make the last sacrifice in attempting to win them to the hope of immortality. Doubtless the whole essence of missionary labour is comprised in this abstract idea; nor can it be imagined that any who go forth in this spirit shall be suffered to spend their strength altogether for nought, even though the measures they pursue are so little adapted to the specific character of the work before them, that miracle only could give them extensive success.

"But this elementary notion of evangelical labour assuredly does not include all that ought to occupy the attention of those who engage in the work of propagating Christianity among the heathen. If there are any who, from a jealous fear of the introduction of a secular spirit, would affirm that nothing ought to belong to a Christian mission but the bare announcement of salvation, such persons might instantly be convicted of a practical inconsistency; for which of them is there that would not strive, in conveying religious instruction, to adapt both his language and his argument to the capacity and disposition of those to whom he speaks? Who would be so absurd as to exhort a child and an adult, a peasant and a scholar, to repentance and faith, precisely in the same terms? None, in fact, would carry their theoretical contempt of human wisdom to this point of extravagance. Common sense, not soon put quite to silence, leads even the most determined dogmatists to conform themselves, as nearly as they can, to the intellectual condition—to the ignorance, or to the known prejudices of those to whom they announce the Gospel.

"But this adaptation of the style to the hearer contains, by implication, an apology for the use of all those subsidiary means which I have to plead for as essential to the completeness of a Christian mission to the heathen. If the actual condition of the people we are attempting to convert is known—and it ought always to be known before we make the attempt,—then a mission to that people must include *a peculiarity of means*, that must make the outfit utterly inappropriate to any other destination.

"Can any one blame this adaptation of means to special ends, who himself uses persuasion at all? for in doing so he plainly recognises the principle, that a part is assigned to the skill and intelligence of the agent in the Divine economy of salvation. Having gone so far, he can with no reason stop short in half measures; or after himself using discretion and skill in the business of Christian instruction, find fault with those who employ *any means*, how elaborate or circuitous soever they may seem, which appear to have a tendency to facilitate the entrance or progress of religion. In a word, if Christians feel themselves bound, by the most solemn obligation, to preach the Gospel wherever they can gain a hearing, they are also bound, by the very same responsibility, to bring into the service, not only their zeal and piety, but all the sagacity, and skill, and knowledge they possess, or may acquire. To contemn any probable means of accomplishing their great object, is in fact to spurn the sanctions under which they act. If, for example, a plan were proposed, which should recommend itself by its obvious reasonableness, Christians would have no more liberty to reject it, than they have to withdraw altogether from the missionary enterprise. The duty of preaching the Gospel contains the duty of doing so in the best manner we are able.

"If the work of evangelizing the nations were held to consist simply in finding men of devoted piety, in fitting them out, and shipping them away to distant shores, as the winds of heaven may determine;—if the missionary work be nothing more than the casting the good seed at random over the earth, then indeed we must grant that counsel, and concert, and knowledge, and special qualification, can add little or nothing to the hope of success; and then, those who are the least esteemed in the Church for wisdom, or least distinguished by acquirements, may, as well as the most accomplished, assume the reins of management.

"A few years ago, this inartificial notion of missions might perhaps have found a multitude of advocates among the pious. But the rebukes of experience have now rendered it almost obsolete. All intelligent and well-informed persons have become thoroughly convinced that, so long as our missionaries go not forth armed with miraculous powers, they must encounter difficulties which can be surmounted only by special qualities of mind, in addition to piety, courage, and devotedness. It is ascertained, also, that the necessary qualifications of a missionary are, in part, the gifts of nature to here and there an individual, and in part must be the result of a long and laborious training."

Within our narrow limits it were utterly impracticable to enter into the wide field which the varied topics contained in, or suggested by this long passage are calculated to open up for investigation and discussion. All, therefore, that can be attempted, is to offer a few practical remarks on some of the leading points.

What, then, with a special reference to India, is the great object which, as Christian philanthropists, we ought ever to avow? The grand ultimate object we ought unceasingly to avow is,—*the intellectual, moral, and spiritual regeneration of the universal mind*;—or, *in the speediest and most effectual manner, the reaching and vitally imbuing the entire body of the people with the leaven of Gospel truth.* Nothing short of this consummation, as *our grand end*, ought we ever to recognise;—and in proportion to the magnitude of the end ought to be the number, and variety, and energy of our operations. The object being thus defined, the question next arises, How, or by what specific means is it best to be accomplished?—How, or in what way can the Gospel be most speedily and effectually brought to bear on the entire mass of the people? Looking at the history of the past, we may say, that by common consent, there are *three generic modes* of applying it. There is, first, ***the preaching of the Gospel to adults***; secondly, ***the teaching of it to the young***; and, thirdly, the ***translation and circulation of the Bible and other religious works.***

These may be regarded as the three primary measures for the practical application of the weapon of evangelical truth. Of the abstract propriety of resorting to one and all of these methods, no intelligent Christian has ever entertained a doubt. The reasoning applicable to each is as simple as it is conclusive. God has already given efficacy to the preaching of the word; He has promised to do so to the end of the world; let therefore the word be faithfully preached at the seasons, and in the manner best suited to the circumstances and capacities of the hearers. God has already smiled propitious on the diligent prayerful training of the young; He has promised always to bless such training; let therefore the young receive the rudiments, and the more mature the higher principles of useful and religious knowledge, in the way which experience proves to be best adapted to secure the desired end. God has already blessed the reading of the Scripture; He hath promised that His word shall never return unto Him void; let the Bible therefore be circulated in the mode most eligible, and to the extent most practicable. Thus far, all who sincerely profess the Christian faith ought to be agreed.

How unwise, then, how injurious, how almost impious is it, to pitch these means against each other?—Preaching against Education; or the circulation of the Bible against either?—as if they were mutual antagonists, instead of being, what they truly are, mutual friends and allies? What are they, but different methods for accomplishing the same end?—different modes of bringing the Gospel-instrumentality into contact with the minds of different classes of human beings? Happily, on the last of these measures little difference of opinion has arisen among the friends of missions;—but how often has education been unhappily represented as somehow opposed to the preaching of the Gospel? If, indeed, by education were meant what is ***merely***

schools for the young. Again, in such a country as China, where multitudes are taught to read, but from which all foreigners who might educate the young or preach to adults are systematically excluded, the circulation of the Bible seems the only expedient to which Christians can, in the first instance, resort. And even in a country like India, where numbers have learned to read, and where young and old are more or less accessible to instruction, there may be differences of opinion as to *the relative prominence* that is due to the respective measures so long as society is only in a *transition state*,—the *proportion* of interest, and resources, and labour that should be lavished on each,—and the *distinctive* form which each must assume from peculiarities of climate, locality, and government; as well as the social, religious, and hereditary opinions, habits, and prejudices of the people. At certain stages, also, of the further progress of society towards a more elevated state of refined enjoyment, the *practicability* of different plans which tend to accelerate the progression, must vary with the parts which have already sent forth the most vigorous shoots, and the ability to meet efficiently the peculiar exigencies of each. Hence may arise fresh differences of opinion as to the necessity and expediency of modifying former measures, and as to the best ways of adapting these to the flux and reflux of circumstances. From these generalities we now proceed to offer some remarks on certain leading points involved in the three great measures for conducting the work of evangelization, beginning with the CHRISTIAN EDUCATION SCHEME.

Connected with this scheme, the single topic of incalculable importance in practice, on which we wish, if possible, to fasten attention, may be announced in the following terms:—

Since the young, composing as they do the majority of every people, are destined to become the heads of families, and the leaders of opinion in the next generation; and, since a thorough Christian education must be allowed, on all hands, to be one of the most powerful instruments in demolishing superstition and prejudice, and in training up a race distinguished by intelligence, and, it may be, devoted piety; —what, *in the present heathenish state of things*, is the course of instruction that ought to be pursued with the clearest prospect of speedy and triumphant success? Ought it to be *limited in kind and in degree*, so as to admit of being spread, *at the same expense of means*, over a *wider* surface, and rendered available to a *greater* mass of the juvenile population? Or, ought it to be *multiplied in kind and increased in degree*; and, consequently, be restricted to a *narrower* sphere, and a more *select* number, with the view of ultimately and more speedily reaching the *entire mass*, through the instrumentality of those awakened and enlightened? In other words,—is it better to pursue the *direct* method of attempting at once to impart *a general elementary knowledge* to the *many*; or the *indirect* method of attempting to reach the *many* through the agency of the instructed *few*?

Each of these methods has had its advocates; each has now been tried in different parts of India with various success. Judging, however, from past facts and appearances, we may safely aver, that till of late the friends of Christianity in India have in a great measure, and with two or three exceptions, adopted and patronized the more limited or elementary course of instruction—partly from its being unavoidable at the *commencement*, and partly from its *apparent directness of application* to the great body of the people. In other words, their efforts seem to have been chiefly confined to the *general elementary instruction* of children, or youths much below the age of puberty. But is this the best mode of attaining the great end proposed? And are those means necessarily the best, which from their apparent directness of application may, *at first view*, promise to be the most efficacious? Or, supposing the mode and the means to be the best and most practicable at the outset, does it follow that they must always continue to be so? As we are compelled to answer in the negative, it now devolves upon us to adduce satisfactory reasons.

Here it may be premised that, as regards any plan which may have for its object *the direct instruction of the mass of the people*, we must at once be struck with the consideration, that all the combined resources of Christian benevolence at present are, and must ever be, incommensurate with the vastness of the undertaking. This the advocates of general elementary instruction are willing to admit. They scruple not to avow, that the disproportion between the means and the object contemplated, is truly appalling. Yet they console themselves with the hope, that to the extent to which the field is occupied, real good is effected. But what is this good? What is the nature and amount? And how produced?

These are questions which, we believe, numbers of the supporters of Christian missions seldom think of asking in a scrutinizing intelligible form. And yet the importance of the result to which a proper answer would lead,—either as defending the propriety of present plans from the desultory attacks of some, and the systematic opposition of others; or as establishing the desireableness of a change of measures by which a more efficient direction might be given to our resources in money and influence,—is enough to challenge an investigation.

The truth is, that when the intelligence is conveyed that several schools have been organized, that large numbers of youth are in regular attendance, and that small portions of the Christian Scriptures are daily read, the good people at home and in India generally rest content,—not because of indifference or apathy, but because of easy incurious self-complacency. They immediately conclude that much good is doing, and they are predisposed to expect still more; without any very *definite* notion of what the good is, or of the process by which it has been, or is to be, brought about. Or if the subject be allowed to excite a temporary share of curiosity and reflection, the mind would appear to be satisfied with some loose and vague notions respecting the change which the gift of reading, and especially the ability to read sacred books, must *some how or other* produce on the rising generation, in the way of disarming prejudice, and creating a thirst after knowledge, which may eventually prove of the utmost advantage to the rapid spread of Christianity. Nay! there often lingers an indefinite impression that those who in early youth have been taught to peruse portions of the Bible,—even though these should be perused with much the same kind of feeling as would be the fragments of a Puranic tale, and though the tuition should be conducted as it has hitherto been, *in nine cases out of ten*, under a *heathen master*,—must surely in manhood openly avow themselves followers of the Cross.

That an elementary education may qualify for the common business of a humble life—that it may, in some instances, render certain terms familiar, which, on account of their strangeness, always prove repulsive to the adult or wholly uneducated, when addressed directly on the solemn truths of religion,—and that in these respects, something has already been achieved, may readily be acknowledged. But that any decided permanent change in the *national intellect*, any real diminution of prejudice or of attachment to established forms, or of resistance to the reception of a holier faith, can, to any great extent, be traced to, or reasonably expected to result from such a course of education, it would require a sacrifice of judgment to enthusiasm to believe.

Let the matter be coolly and rationally examined; let evidence be weighed; let due deference be paid to the voice of experience; let the constitution, or successions of state in the human mind be attended to.—Admit that thousands of children are initiated into the elements of education—that they can read ordinary books, write with tolerable ease, and cast accounts with creditable facility, and that much of what *we* may deem surpassing in beauty and utility, has been accurately committed to memory:—*and what is the result?* Is it a result fraught with benefits superior in kind and lasting in duration? How much of what has been imparted to *the boy, at no small expense, will possess a vivifying, regenerating influence?* How much will fixedly cling to, and permanently influence the conduct and character of *the man?* Generally, nothing at all beyond the artificial or mechanical parts of the acquisition—nothing save the ability to read, write, or apply to the cases of petty dealing, the simplest rules of arithmetic. The boy is positively too young to imbibe, and the instruction received too meagre to impart, any vital principle which can keep even the knowledge acquired fresh upon the memory; or can create that inextinguishable curiosity which will not be allayed till the means of gratification are secured. And, if his own mind has not attained to that standard of proficiency which will be of material benefit to himself, how is it possible for any influence to emanate from him that will produce the slightest impression on the surrounding multitudes?

It is unfair to judge of this subject by a reference to the state of things in Great Britain; though such reference, *properly made*, may aid the conceptions of those whose circumstances have not enabled them visibly to perceive the difference.

Now, in Great Britain, what is the usual effect of a mere elementary education; such as that communicated in a *common village* school? Is there any thing ordinarily conveyed, which, as a literary acquisition, can raise an individual to an eminence above his fellows, by widening the narrow circle within which his thoughts and sentiments would naturally revolve? Or, is there any thing conveyed which can excite a hearty desire to pursue the study of literature and science, with the view of enlarging his own mind, and benefiting the community in which he moves? It must be seldom indeed, we presume, that at a village school such knowledge can be acquired, or such ardent desires awakened. And why?—because from the immaturity of the habit of reflection, much of what is read does not cleave to the mind as *digested* knowledge—knowledge incorporated, as it were, with the very substance of mind, and forming the staple of thought:—because from the meagreness of the acquisition itself viewed in combination with this cause, the mind does not, and cannot obtain, that *tasting* of literature and science which would inevitably insure an increasing appetite for more.

But it may be said, that in the case of the great body of the people there is nothing to render it an object in itself particularly desirable that *many* should attain to an intellectual superiority which might enable them to exert a personal influence on those around—that it is quite enough, if, by being taught to read, they are endowed with the ability to peruse and understand that precious volume which conveys the knowledge that "maketh man wise unto salvation." Without at present disputing the sufficiency of this endowment in a land where the Bible is believed and read almost by all, let us attend to its own independent effects, not when left unexercised, but when cultivated with diligence and unceasing care. Let us refer to those who, with heart and soul, are engaged in the work of communicating the rudiments not only of secular but of religious knowledge to British youth; and what is the constant burden of their complaint—the one note of lamentation, that is never out of tune?—Is it not the meagre appearance of fruit as the result of all their devoted labours? And what is the source of their encouragement to persevere in a task apparently so toilsome and profitless?—Is it not the hope of realizing some *distant ultimate* benefit? Whence is this remote benefit expected to arise? Is it from the *sole* unaided power of surviving impressions of early education? Scarcely ever. It is mainly from the expectation that individuals so taught may, in after-life, be situated among those whose sentiments and example,—tallying with instructions formerly delivered, and practices formerly recommended,—may reawaken and call forth into lively exercise principles of thought and action that had been imbibed in youth, but had lain dormant in the secret chambers of the soul. And it is *chiefly* on account of the greater facility with which, in such cases, sound impressions may be produced and deepened by the general influences that ever radiate from, and circulate amongst the members of a well-ordered and well-cultivated society, that the propriety of bestowing early culture however limited, is defended, and its actual bestowment proved to be more or less advantageous.

If, then, in a land where every circumstance is favourable

to the growth of what is noble and generous—in a land where the reciprocation of enlightened opinions is free as the air of heaven—in a land where the sacred and civil institutions, the improved manners and customs, the records and traditions of centuries, the associations and pastimes of infancy, and, above all, the religious faith and observances of the people —all *fully harmonize* with the elementary knowledge, literary and religious, that is imparted :—and if, with these incalculable advantages, such knowledge,—*apart from after means of improvement, or those external, social, and spiritual influences which quicken and mature*,—generally fails in producing those decided changes that would materially affect the individual himself, or ameliorate the condition of society :—who, that has any pretensions to a reflecting mind, may not discern the utter powerlessness of such elementary knowledge, literary and religious, in operating the anticipated changes, in a country where that knowledge, *instead of fully harmonizing*, is found to run *counter* to all the institutions, manners, customs, habits, rites, ceremonies, traditions, metaphysical and religious opinions of the whole mass of the people ?—in a country too, where, *as yet*, there scarcely exist any of those *after* means of quickening latent energies, of developing the seeds of latent knowledge—any of those reviving influences which issue from, and healthfully play around the entire fabric of a well-regulated community ?

Will it still be objected by some, that all this is mere theorizing ? It may ; but we would urge, yea, beseech them to reconsider the matter; and see whether it be not rather a legitimate deduction from unquestionable facts. And should any doubt yet remain, we would appeal to a circumstance too weighty to be overlooked, and too conclusive to admit of evasion. Why is it that so many *eye-witnesses complain* of the littleness of visible effect arising from the institution and multiplication of *elementary* schools ? Allowing the efficacy which issues in *conversion* to be wholly beyond, and that which issues in mere *intellectual* or other temporal improvement, to be to a great extent, within the control of human agency, why do we hear so many sincere friends of the Christian cause *mar-*

vel, that no positive change towards a better condition of society has appeared from the extensive educationary operations which have been conducted under Christian management for the last forty years? Is not every expression of wonder on the part of those who have the means of judging, conclusive testimony as to the certainty of the fact, that no change has yet been effected by the operations in question, which bears a just proportion to the time and means already expended? And does not the preceding view afford the most natural, if not the only adequate explanation of the fact? Again, we say, let the subject be duly pondered; let it be contemplated in all its bearings; let the sand-like character of the youthful mind be considered—its levity, its instability, its light-hearted carelessness; let the meagreness of the knowledge and the insufficiency of the mode in which even that little is imparted be steadily kept in view; more especially, let the meditative spirit dwell on the circumstance, that whatever instruction is *in the first instance* conveyed, flows unmixed in one distinct channel; and that all the feelings, sentiments, and actions of old and young, among the people, flow unremoved and unamalgamated in another channel essentially separated from the former:—and, instead of greatly marvelling that the aspect of society has not undergone more important changes, we may well be filled with astonishment at the want of sagacity or unreasonableness of those, who could seriously expect changes so great and so decisive to result from causes so utterly inadequate. The ingredients that unite in swelling the current which flows in each channel, exhibit in one respect the peculiar property of those substances that possess no chemical affinity—those substances that are not only mutually distinct, but mutually repulsive of each other. And if it be held an object of importance wholly to displace that which has the preoccupancy, it can never be effected by the application of a small portion of antagonist ingredients—as these might float innocuously on the surface. If effected at all, the one must be gradually dislodged by a corresponding increase in the volume of the other. That, in the case of education as hitherto generally conducted in India, this increase has yet been sufficient, is widely remote of the truth. For it is wholly incredible that mere elementary instruction, communicated under numberless disadvantages, can ever bear any reasonable proportion to the stupendous mass of prejudice and superstition which it is intended to remove or destroy.

Nor is the good effected by such a limited system simply partial in its nature and contracted in its extent; it is very uncertain in its *duration*. Imagine a case in our own highly-favoured land. Suppose that from some of those almost subterranean caverns in the heart of our great cities, where ignorance, vice, and profanity reign with unchecked dominion, hundreds of youth, no matter from what motives, are induced to attend one of our elementary Christian schools:—suppose that, during the period of their attendance, they are exposed, evening and morning, at home, to all the brutalizing influences of unhallowed lips and profligate examples:—suppose that, after one or two years, at the early age of six, seven, eight, or nine, they are all removed from school, and again wholly shut up within the haunts of ungodliness and immorality; no more accessible to the warning voice of the teacher, or the preacher, or any Christian friend:—what impression could we *ordinarily* expect to be conveyed to them at so tender an age, in such adverse circumstances, which would cling to them in after-life, in spite of the unopposed host of corrupting temptations, and seductive allurements to folly, sin, and shame? And yet this is but a faint and feeble picture of the real condition of the great majority of elementary mission schools in India. Hundreds and thousands of children may, from various motives, be induced to attend; at home they are encompassed with the demoralizing influences of a loathsome superstition; after an attendance of one or two years, they are withdrawn from school; they then replunge into the dead sea of an abominable heathenism; are swallowed up in it; and, for the most part, no more heard of by those who would gladly guide them towards Zion. What *lasting* impression can, in such circumstances, be expected to be communicated? We are aware, that there are occasional instances of persons who, in youth happened to receive an elementary education, having in riper years become converts to the Christian faith. But in these cases, it were a glaring misapprehension of the real nature of the facts to attribute the enlightened reception of Christianity, as an effect, to the elementary education, as the proximate instrumental cause. The lines have fallen to these individuals in more pleasant places. By the working of a gracious Providence, they have for a season escaped as it were from the vortex of heathen society, and, during that time, have come in contact with some of the people of God—and from these has emanated an influence which has been blessed in subduing the souls of the wanderers to the Saviour. All such cases, instead of proving the inherent power of rudimental instruction in effecting great changes on character, only furnish an admirable illustration of the efficacy of *after social and spiritual influences*, to awaken into life and enshrine with the glories of true light and liberty. The real question then is this:—Of all the thousands of youths who have received a mere elementary education, how many have, *in consequence, and solely in consequence of it*, contributed in after-life to the diffusion of free and enlightened sentiments? How many have lent a more favourable ear to the announcement of the glad tidings? How many have become "burning and shining lights?" How many would be found able and disposed to uphold even the present inadequate supply, in the event of European agents and influence being wholly withdrawn? We fear that the most boundless charity would weep over the scantiness of the catalogue. Indeed, so long as there is no living principle infused to maintain life, and no active leaven to quicken the dull sluggish mass, things must in a great measure remain at once stationary, and absolutely dependent on *foreign* aid—aid which, from its very nature, must ever be feeble and precarious. And should no change of plans be sanctioned by the Legislative Almoners of Christian benevolence at home, the hands of the Executive in India must continue bound as with iron fetters, and the state of mental imbecility and childhood, so far as the cause in question shall operate, must be perpetuated from age to age. After the removal of a thousand generations, and the profuse expenditure of thousands of lives, and tens of thousands of gold and silver, we might look around for fruit, without discerning any to regale the eyes, or to cheer the heart;—and even then might the sudden removal of foreign agency be the signal for a speedy and general relapse.

This state of things suggests to us an extreme, but somewhat analogous case. In a country wholly destitute of indigenous forests, a new colony is planted. The soil is naturally excellent, and by proper cultivation may be made to bear the most useful products of foreign climes. Among others, the seeds of trees of different species are transported and deposited in the earth; they soon germinate and grow. But the country is excessively cold, and the foreign supply of large timber being barely sufficient for ship-building, machinery, &c., *all* the young and rising plants are successively cut down for fire-wood; none are allowed to attain to the maturity of growth that is necessary for bearing fruit. At length, by some rupture among the nations, or some disastrous inroad of nature's elements, all supplies from abroad are cut off. Must not the general misery of the people be inevitable? Certainly. And yet, had prudence and judgment guided their counsels, and directed their efforts, instead of a limited and precarious supply from abroad, they might have had numbers of seed-bearing trees that would soon reproduce and multiply their kind a thousandfold; and at no very remote period, meet or even exceed every possible demand, and thus render the inhabitants independent of all future contingencies.

From the whole train of the preceding remarks, what conclusion ought to be drawn? Is it not this,—That *in present circumstances*, all efforts which may be confined to the *direct* method of diffusing *mere elementary* knowledge among the *dense mass* of the heathen youth of India must be very inadequate; and, if *exclusively* pursued, can entail little else than expense, failure, and disappointment. Hence, much of the unfruitfulness of the system of elementary instruction which, from various causes, in many respects unavoidable, has hitherto been chiefly prosecuted in mission schools ;—a system, occupying a sphere so very limited, as scarcely to embrace any of those higher objects, without the attainment of which, all previous advantages are comparatively lost,—the youthful plants, from the premature abandonment of them, not being allowed to fructify and grow into strength, and shoot out into the heavens their wide-spreading boughs. Hence the frank and ready acknowledgment made of late years by so many who have had the benefit of experience; and the corresponding determination to bend a more special attention towards the *indirect* method of imparting that life and strength to the *few*, which will at once impel and enable them to exert a potent influence over the *many*. Hence the persuasion that we ought no longer to rest satisfied with the thought of conferring some limited uncertain benefit, and carelessly indulge the hope of producing some future undefined good ;—that, after surveying the field, and taking reason and experience for our guides, we ought to confess, that to *restrict* ourselves to the spread of elementary knowledge, is in great measure a fruitless waste of our time, our strength, and our pecuniary resources ; since any doubtful good which may be immediately produced must terminate in and perish with the individual.—Hence the growing persuasion that, since our design is to reach most speedily, efficiently, and permanently the great mass of the people, we ought openly to avow the *chief means* to be, so far as regards education, not the elementary instruction of the youth at large, but the raising up and qualifying a body of special agents, whose minds, from the length and variety of their studies might be quickened, expanded, and enlightened. In every individual in whom we thus concentrate the rays of a higher knowledge, we provide a new source whence shall emanate and diverge the rays of quickening truth, to vivify and illume all within the reach of its influence. And if all who are thus taught do not engage *directly* in the work of disseminating true knowledge among their countrymen, they cannot fail to teach extensively by their example,—to imprint a new character on their own children,—and to encourage and support the adoption of any measures that may have for their object the diffusion of sound and enlarged sentiment.

Were the friends of missions, therefore, regularly to inquire, How many young men are engaged in a course of study in the higher departments of knowledge?—instead of, How many children are receiving instruction in the elementary schools?—they would undoubtedly find in the answer to the former inquiry, by much the surer test of the present and prospective advancement of the Hindus. Indeed, so strong is our conviction on this subject, that we do not hesitate to say, that it would augur more for the real welfare of India, were ten privileged to receive the higher instruction, rather than a thousand admitted to the elementary schools. Do we then disapprove of the organization of schools of the latter description? Quite the contrary. In the face of all opposition, we would again and again reiterate the statement, that, *in the first instance*, such schools must be instituted. But it is one thing to assert the necessity of *preparatory* measures, and quite another to rest in these as an *ultimate end*. This were indeed a humiliation of judgment. If the condition of society be such, that few or none of the young are at once qualified and willing to enter on a course of higher study, what expedient can be devised, save that of opening initiatory schools, in which the proper qualifications may be acquired? But would it indicate much wisdom to stop here, and expend in wasteful extravagance our resources on the subordinate object? With very limited means at our disposal compared with the exigencies of the case, we should value and support inferior schools, principally on account of their auxiliary connection with a higher seminary;—and, whenever that connection ceases to exist, and the elementary school forms no longer one of the nurseries of a superior institution, we should certainly hesitate to expend much on its continuance. Between the two grades of institution, there would be a reciprocal action and reaction. While the lower supplied the higher with disciplined pupils, the higher would tend to infuse new life into the lower. As vacancies in the former would be filled up by pupils selected from the latter on account of their proficiency, this constant removal of those who distinguish themselves to enjoy the benefit of a superior education, would operate as a powerful and salutary stimulus throughout the entire system. Wholesome emulation would thereby be excited; increased exertion would ensue; and greater sacrifices would be made by parents and guardians to insure the regularity and prolong the period of attendance. Indeed, when the advantages consequent on a course of study in the higher institution began to be understood by a community rapidly growing in intelligence, the requisite qualifications for admission might often be exacted without our incurring the previous trouble and expense of communicating them.

To sum up the whole in a few words:—From a full and comprehensive view of the nature and constitution of man, specially as modified by the Brahmanical system;—from the feebleness of impression on the youthful mind in matters that require abstract thought, or tend vitally to affect, and permanently to change the heart;—from the buoyant restlessness of the Hindu character;—from the obliterating and stupifying tendency of the countless abominations of heathenism;—from the pressing wants and growing necessities of a society newly awakening from the torpor of a long and dreary night;—from the lessons of a past experience, which present little else than a catalogue of failures to warn and instruct;—from these and other circumstances which might be indefinitely enlarged upon, it must be adjudged essential,—towards securing the full benefits of a Christian educational course,—that, above and beyond the mere elementary schools, separate institutions should be founded for the express purpose of turning the former to full account,—for the express purpose of communicating that higher knowledge in every department of literature, science, and theology, the possession of which, with the divine blessing, naturally tends to stamp, and permanently to fix the character,—for the express purpose of preventing many a promising plant from being exposed to every rude blast and every scorching ray, instead of being transferred to a more genial soil and a more kindly atmosphere, where its roots might spread, and its branches wave defiance to every tempest. *In the present condition of the people of India, one such central seminary, of a higher grade, with its attendant retinue of preparatory gymnasia, would do more towards vitally impressing the intellect and heart of the people, and consequently towards furthering the great cause of national regeneration, than any number of mere elementary schools, however indefinitely*

Dismissing for the present the subject of education, we come to the next primary measure, or that of PREACHING. The Gospel, it has been again and again remarked, *must be preached* to the *adult* population. In doing so, we are not only warranted, but invited to look for a plentiful effusion of God's Holy Spirit to crown the proclamation with the desired increase.

Connected with this theme, the question of vast practical moment,—the question of questions,—which we mean to start and consider, is, *Who are, or ought to be the preachers?*

Making every allowance for individual opinions, occasionally expressed in written journals, or oral addresses—for desultory and ephemeral measures, or even for a few isolated systematic attempts, on the part of societies or their agents,—it cannot be doubted that, in the spirit and working of the modern missionary system as a whole, the reigning principle has generally been to look almost exclusively to the Churches at home for the continuous supply of superiorly qualified labourers. This ought now to be regarded as a fundamental error. It must not, however, be imputed to any man, or body of men, as blameworthy. Quite the contrary. It arose partly from inattention to the means employed in propagating Christianity in past ages; partly from inconsideration as to the capabilities of foreign agents, and the peculiarities of the Heathen mind; partly from inexperience of the specific necessities of the field to be brought under cultivation; partly from the hereditary opinions and prepossessions of numbers of the friends and supporters of the missionary cause; and partly from the frequent impossibility of acting otherwise in the earlier stages of the evangelistic process throughout the different nations of the earth.

But the time has now come when, from the calm and dispassionate review of the past and present state of missions, we may, in reference to the source whence labourers ought to be drawn, be allowed to insist on the systematic adoption of an entirely opposite principle as the paramount one. In other words, instead of any longer looking solely or chiefly to the British and other Christian Churches not only for the original but the continuous supply of labourers, we ought now to say, Look to *these Churches* for the *original* supply of labourers to communicate the first impulse; but let these give that shape and direction to their operations which may most speedily cause *the field itself* to send forth the *continuous* supply.

Unimportant as this distinction may appear, the steady observance of it would lead to the mightiest practical results. Were the latter principle to gain the ascendant in missionary counsels and plans, it would soon lead to a remodelling of the framework of the general system. It would furnish an entirely new test and criterion of the success of missions. Looking always to home, and dependent on it for a succession of labourers, the prevailing object seems hitherto to have been to secure as *many ordinary* converts as possible—to report as many in the list of baptized and communicants, as possible. Now, *mere numbers* furnish no valid test of the really flourishing state of any mission. Look at that gorgeous exotic from a sunny clime! How proudly it rears its majestic stem, and shoots out its magnificent foliage, and displays its dazzling hues, as if in derision of the flora of these northern realms!—How it flourishes! Yes; it flourishes well in the hot-house of a botanic garden,

—but can it be said to flourish well in Scotland? No; not unless it became so naturalized, that, like an indigenous plant, it could thrive independent of shelter or artificial heat; and could maintain its native vigour, in spite of frost and snow. So with a mission in any heathen land! Our eyes are turned to schools where the Gospel is taught,—to chapels where it is preached. The spot is a Goshen in a land of moral darkness; and, like Goshen of old, freed also it may be from the plagues and the pestilences that smite and destroy the surrounding multitudes. Behold, how Christianity flourishes! Yes, it flourishes well in that garden, under the nurturing care, and vivifying warmth, of Christian missionaries. But can it be said to flourish in India? No, not unless it become so naturalized, and have taken such deep root in the soil, that it can flourish and perpetuate itself, independent of foreign aid. That a mission has succeeded in working out for itself the means of *self-support* and *self-propagation*:— This, this is the only valid test of real permanent success!

Tell us of a station where thousands of ordinary converts are reported, but not one capable of acting the part of an independent propagator of Christianity, and we must say, that that mission, with reference to the present and more especially the future, cannot be said to be in a flourishing state. Tell us of another station, which can report no such thousands, but can point to a few capable of acting the part of evangelists—and that station we must pronounce to be in a flourishing state. As regards the vitality and permanency of Christianity, the mission which, with the Divine blessing, raises up a few propagators, has done more than one which counts thousands who require all their own diligence, and the superadded vigilance of devoted foreigners, to keep alive the flickering spark in their own breasts. As regards eternity, a hundred souls are more precious than one;—as regards the intrinsic worth of a soul, that of one feeble in the faith is as valuable as that of anyone strong in the faith. But, as regards the country at large, and the welfare of its inhabitants, one convert strong in the faith,—able to sustain the life in himself, and communicate it to others,—is worth a hundred or a thousand ordinary disciples. The soul of the humblest and most illiterate peasant may be as precious in the sight of God, as the soul of the most powerful in intellect, and the most advanced in spiritual gifts and attainments. But as regards the great interests of a realm, (say Scotland,) one Knox is worth ten thousand illiterate peasants. And the institution which might be honoured in rearing a Knox, would do more for Christianity and mankind, than if it brought ten thousand undisciplined peasants into the fold. The influence of the former extends far and wide in space, and propagates itself onwards along the roll of ages, vitally affecting the destinies of successive generations. The influence of the latter might, in a great measure, be confined to themselves, and perish with themselves. In missions, that one which is still dependent on home for labourers, has got no permanent footing, and is no better than a sickly exotic which will droop, the moment it is left to itself and its own inherent powers. Left to itself in such a mission, Christianity might, in the course of a single generation, decline into the feebleness of old age ; and, in the next, from the corruptions and interblendings of it with surrounding heathenism, new heresies might spring up—the foul but stable monuments of its short-lived reign. It is not enough that in any mission there should be individuals known under the *name* of native teachers, catechists, or preachers. For what is a name without the possession of some corresponding substantial reality ? To ascertain the real value of native functionaries, we must ask the question,—How many of these would proceed with their labours of love, were the vigilant superintendence, and animating example, and stirring encouragement, and pecuniary recompense of European missionaries suddenly and wholly withdrawn ? How many would unflinchingly persevere in their holy calling, if wholly abandoned to themselves and their own resources ? Alas ! how often would a faithful answer to this question reduce almost to nothingness even the present sorry catalogue of native labourers ! But how can we call those native labourers really worthy of the name, who are destitute of the mental and spiritual qualifications and heroic zeal which would carry them forward, supposing all European missionaries were removed in a day? However conspicuous the figure which *numbers* may make in statistical columns, how can we call any mission flourishing which has not succeeded in raising up at least a few converts endowed with those powers, gracious and acquired, that would embolden them to persevere, in the face of desertion and danger, in an independent course of labour?

Leaving these generalities, we proceed next to exhibit, from a variety of special considerations, the necessity of making the rearing of qualified natives a primary, and not a secondary or subordinate department of missionary labour in India.

Supposing that the present missionary stations in India bore, numerically, a far greater proportion to its necessities than they really do, how are they supplied with agents? Is the supply adequate to the demand at the stations themselves? By no means. For years past, in Eastern India, almost all the central and branch missions of the great English societies may be said to be stationary. How is this? Chiefly from the inadequate supply of European missionaries. There is scarcely a settlement which can, at this moment, afford to act on the aggressive, in effectually widening the circle of light into the circumjacent territory, without subtracting so much from its own limited efficiency. Few as are the stations that have been already formed, the services of even one labourer could not be dispensed with for a season, however short, without leaving his sphere almost entirely destitute,—a circumstance which, in the present stage of improvement, would be tantamount to a total abandonment of the work already accomplished. For it is not in an infantine state of things, as it is in those more highly favoured lands where vital, self-sustaining, self-propagating principles have long been implanted, and have taken firm and deep root. At home, for example, the spiritual labourer may retire for a season, and, returning again, may find his

adding, moreover, how overawed the besieged had been, because they did not venture, as before, openly to issue forth to attack them in the open field. Thus, year after year, the attack may be renewed, and the report brought back of similar success. In the course of a century, there may be a succession of a hundred attacks, a hundred breaches effected in the outer ramparts, and a hundred reports of the wondrous exploits;—and at the end of the hundred years, the fort may be as nearly on the eve of capture and subjugation as at the beginning! So it may fare with the scheme of occasional or unfrequent itineracies,—when never followed up by permanent ministrations. Their history may consist of a monotonous record of deep impressions once made and, it may be, annually renewed—deep impressions, but no real conquest, either temporary or permanent. Hence it is that nothing can well be more unsound or unsafe than to adopt a certain platform calculus; and, by an assumed and arbitrary equation, measure the amount of good effected by the number of isolated impressions reported in the narrative of a long itineracy.

This is not all. It is not merely that occasional impressions, altogether remote from the daily current of human thought and feeling, must, in the overwhelming majority of instances, prove fleeting and unstable,—terminating in little or no real and lasting good. In a heathen country like India, should transitory visitations leave at any time behind them some seeds of truth, which, in individual cases, may fructify,—has the grave, the momentous consideration been sufficiently attended to, namely, that unintentionally there may be also implanted the seeds of much positive evil, which, sprouting with the tropical rapidity so characteristic of the growth of error, may inflict essential damage on the best of causes?

Let us draw one illustration of this from the medium of instruction. That medium is, of course, foreign to the European itinerant. Now let us suppose,—what cannot be alleged in favour of one out of ten,—that he has a perfect mastery over the provincial dialect; as well as an intimate acquaintance with human nature in the abstract, and human nature as modified by Hindu institutions. The dialect may contain no analogous terms to express some of the more spiritual doctrines of Christianity. If not, foreign terms must be introduced; or new ones coined; or equivalent ones borrowed or compounded from the Sanskrit. In either case, how formidable the difficulty presented at the very outset of the process of instruction! And yet that difficulty, in the case of a people immersed in grossness,—supersaturated with sensuousness,—is proposed to be overcome in the course of a single address! Or suppose terms somewhat analogous to exist, it may scarcely ever happen that these are identical in import. If not, the confusion and intricacy, instead of being diminished, may even be enhanced;—as it is often far more easy to introduce a new term as the vehicle of a new conception, than to detach from an old term the idea to which it has once been wedded. On this subject we appeal at once to theory and to universal experience. We appeal to all,—who in the hey-day amusements of youth, have employed certain terms in connection with the jovial, the frolicsome, or the ludicrous,—whether, in riper years, the recurrence of the terms does not always insure a recurrence of the early associated ideas—so as to prove like discord to the harmony of sage discourse; to detract from the gravity of venerable usage; and even painfully to tumultuate the very exercises of devotion? We appeal to all—in whose minds the various professions and the ten thousand events and contingencies of life have produced casual associations with terms that are wholly alien to the terms themselves,—whether the same disturbing influences have not been experienced? Apart altogether from such inveterate associations, we appeal to all judges and pleaders, to all preachers and teachers, to all lecturers and speakers, in public and in private—to all, in short, who have exerted any degree of discrimination in their intercourse with their fellow-men, whether, even in cases where there is a community of speech—a reciprocity of information,—an intercommunion of sentiment, the same notion may not often be enunciated by the speaker in one sense, and understood by the hearer in another?—And whether this does not repeatedly happen in cases where the party addressed may be earnestly anxious to be enlightened and improved?

If thus it be at home, what must it be in a region like India? —where the audience may be not only wholly ignorant of the subject of discourse, but wholly disinclined to its announcements, and more or less intolerant of its proposed results?—where, moreover, there may be no natural community of language, nor parity of general knowledge, nor congeniality of sentiment? Above all, what must it be, where almost every term in the entire vocabulary of theology, is preoccupied and appropriated to the embodiment of some idea altogether foreign to the genius and spirit of Christianity?—where every religious term is linked to what is erroneous in faith, idolatrous in worship, blasphemous in principle, or abominable in practice?—and this too, not from the casual association of youthful pastime, nor the incidents of professional engagement, nor the fortuitous coincidences of accident and adventure,—but, from the systematic training of youth and the inveterate habits of manhood, the opinions of the head and the preferences of the heart, the immemorial usage of ancestors, and all the heart-stirring recollections of ages of glory and renown! Take one or two examples as an illustration of the difficulty. Talk to the idolatrous Hindus of *sin*—endeavour to convince of sin, that you may convince of righteousness. Sin is a term of familiar occurrence. But though freely used by both parties, what a discrepancy between the ideas of which it is the common emblem! When you mention sin, yours is the divinely revealed idea. But what can the use of the term suggest to the minds of the hearers, except the idea with which, from infancy, it has been associated as symbol and representative? Will the utterance of a familiar sound from the lips of a stranger, all at once transfuse the new or additional idea which may be latent in his breast? Impossible. The enunciation of the term will at first naturally and inevitably excite in the hearers' mind the very notions—and none other—to which they have all their days been accustomed. And what are these? What is sin? Probably the sin most readily suggested, will be that of *touching something unclean*, or partaking of food that has been handled by one of another caste, or some other imaginary offence still more frivolous. Talk of the necessity of the soul's being *cleansed from all sin*;—and the process of purification suggested, will be that of *ablution* in the Ganges or some other sacred stream. Tell them that without *holiness* no one shall enter the kingdom of heaven;—and the impression conveyed, will be that without *meritorious virtue*, or that excellence which results from the performance of works of merit, or the endurance of ascetic mortification, it is impossible to ascend into any of the heavens of the gods. Proclaim the doctrinal fact, that the soul is now *far off*, alienated, or separated from God;—and their own notion will be apt to be confirmed that the soul is *an individualized portion of the Supreme Brahm*, temporarily severed from his substance and confined within the bonds of a material frame. Dilate on the necessity of the soul's being again brought to God, and of being *united to him* by a true and living faith, in order to the enjoyment of perfect bliss;—and you will be understood as enunciating the fundamental doctrine of their own Pantheism; that to secure final beatitude, the soul must, by firm unshaken devotion and intense abstract contemplation, be *reunited with the essence of the Supreme Spirit*. Expatiate on the *joys of heaven*;—and the mind will at once be filled with the endless round of *sensuous enjoyments* which, in their system, constitute celestial bliss. Discourse of the *Divine Being*,—employ the ordinary term for God,—and the thoughts of the hearers will be thrown adrift among *a multitude of imaginary, false, and subordinate divinities*.—To guard against misconception, prefix or substitute an appellation, expressive of some lofty attribute, such as uncontrolled power and dominion,—and instantly will the attention be directed to *one or other of the supreme gods*, who, in a pre-eminent sense may be the depository of that attribute.—To banish the possibility of such polytheistic confusion, seize at once on that term which is the incommunicable designation of the Divine Being, as contradistinguished from all other gods, superior or inferior,—and instantly you suggest the pantheistic conception of the Supreme Spirit, as *the emanative fount and universally modified essence of all other existences.* Come to some doctrine which you believe to be peculiar to Revelation; tell the people that they must be *regenerated* or *born again*, else they can never "see God." Before you are aware, they may go away saying, "oh there is nothing new or strange here; our own Shastras tell us the same thing; we know and believe that we must be born again; it is our fate to be so." But what do they understand by the expression? It is that they are to be born again and again, in some other form, agreeably to their own system of *transmigration or reiterated births.* To avoid the appearance of countenancing so absurd and pernicious a doctrine, you vary your language, and tell them that there must be a *second birth*,—that they must be *twice born.* Now it so happens that this, and all similar phraseology, is preoccupied. The sons of a Brahman have to undergo various purificatory and initiatory ceremonial rites, before they attain to full Brahmanhood. The last of these is the investiture with the sacred thread; which is followed by the communication of the *Gayatri*, or most sacred verse in the Vedas. This ceremonial constitutes, "religiously and metaphorically, their second birth;" henceforward their distinctive and peculiar appellation is that of the *twice born*, or *regenerated men.* Hence it is that your improved language might only convey the impression that all must become perfect Brahmans, ere they can "see God"—a doctrine to which they would at once assent, inasmuch as none except those who, through the course of transmigration, rise to the exalted grade of perfect Brahmanhood, can attain to that "*divine knowledge*" which is essential to a *reabsorption* into the Supreme Spirit.

But why multiply examples? These are sufficient to illustrate our meaning, when we declare that every native term which the Christian missionary can employ to communicate Divine truth, is already appropriated as the chosen symbol of some counterpart deadly error,—and that to sever these terms from meanings and associations which have been instilled from infancy, and rendered venerable by the usage of an immemorial antiquity,—converting them into the vehicle of pure and spiritual conceptions, wholly alien to the thoughts of a sensuous superstitious people,—must be a task of no ordinary difficulty. Indeed, we consider this as one of the greatest, if not the very greatest, of the more immediate difficulties with which the Herald of the Cross has to contend, when addressing an adult audience of Hindu idolaters. And yet, strange to say, though this be a difficulty which those who have most narrowly scrutinized the workings of their own and other men's minds, will ever be the readiest to pronounce as most formidable,—it is perhaps the difficulty which of all others has in practice been least considered,—least weighed,—and least effectually provided against!

What is the drift of the preceding remarks? Is it to pour contempt on all itineracy? Is it to discourage preaching? God forbid! It is simply to reduce the former within its proper dimensions: it is to lead to a system which may render the latter not a name, a mockery, nor a phantom,—but a reality, a power, and an efficacy. When the preacher, by his address, may have raised misconceptions;—when, through ignorance, prejudice, habit, and early association, the noblest truths may be merged into the most detestable errors—the most marvellous facts into mythological fables;—when the sublimest theism may be transmuted into an atheistic pantheism,—the sublimest doctrines into the grovelling forms of idolatrous belief,—and the purest practices into the enslaving round of degrading superstition—what is the remedy? Or is there any? There is,—and it consists in frequent, patient reiteration; accompanied with varied explanation, similitude, illustration, and argument. But, for this the mere itinerating system can make no adequate provision. In order to insure so indispensable an end, there must be a fixed and stationary ministry. In other words, the localising system must be brought into full operation. Such a system efficiently conducted, would at once demand tens of thousands of labourers. And this again lands us in the necessity of resorting to natives, in a way more efficient, and to an extent vastly greater than has ever yet been contemplated. Will this be denounced as innovation? Innovation! Why, it is only to seize the lyre of experience, and sweep it with the finger of common sense. We plead for itineracy; we plead for preaching. All that we insist on is, that both should, if possible, be perfected. How we long to see the day when both may be so effectually combined, as to lead to a universal process of productive and permanent localisation! How glorious,—if really endowed with the requisite qualifications, and having at our disposal and appointment numbers of native teachers and preachers—how glorious to .traverse the whole land as preaching itinerants! Wherever inquiry might be excited, or impressions made, *there* would we localise a missionary to stimulate the inquiry, heighten the impression, and in every way which wisdom could suggest, or experience confirm, follow up all the advantages already gained. Then would we pass on to another city or district; and there would we, if favoured in like manner with increase from on high, repeat the same process. And after a circling series of stations had thus been planted within reach of concert and co-operation, how cheering would it be to return and revisit them all—strengthening and confirming the churches! This, this would be itineracy of the right stamp,—an itineracy which might not only diffuse, but perpetuate the leaven of Christian principle throughout the land!

Apart altogether from the demonstrable argument of *numbers* in proof of the necessity of raising a supply of native teachers and preachers, there are other considerations, some of primary, and others of secondary importance. Without any special regard to classification, we shall here briefly advert to a few.

When we think of the vast extent of territory to be overtaken, and the tens of thousands required for the task, is it wise to overlook the economical part of missionary statistics? Other things being equal, must not that system be preferred, which contemplates the Christianization of India at the lowest pecuniary expenditure? In accelerating that longed-for result, is it nothing that an effective native agency may be maintained at a *fifth* or *sixth* part of the expense of a European agency of corresponding efficiency? If five or six preachers can be supported in place of one, may we not hope that the means of Christian influence will be diffused and multiplied at a rate five or six fold greater? And would not this alone do much towards turning the balance in favour of native agency?

Again, the missionary who desires to labour with real effect in impressing the adult population, ought to be enabled so to exhibit his entire mode, habits, and tenor of life, that, in his daily walk and conversation,—in his outgoings and incomings,—in his domestic and social dealings,—he might be observed and marked by all around;—that, in this way, the preaching of his lips might be enforced by the tenfold more efficacious preaching of a holy, harmless, and irreproachable example, "seen and read of all men." Now, it requires little reflection to perceive, that in the way of *fully* attaining this grand object, a barrier is interposed by the *exotic* manners and habits of European missionaries. This holds true, more especially, of those modes of living to which experience has compelled the inhabitants of a northern clime to resort;—not for the sake of *comfort*,—for that is a commodity which, in the British sense of the term, is unknown in tropical climes,—but simply to insure some portion of health and efficiency for the discharge of necessary duties;—not for the sake of enjoying the fabled luxuries of the East,—for what would be luxuries at home, can *there* be only said to be so many artificial contrivances to obtain some abatement of positive suffering,—so many ingenious expedients, not so much to render life pleasurable, as to make bare existence possible. All such manners, habits, and

der the "injunctions" of the apostles, to betake themselves to the use of ordinary means for rearing and perpetuating a succession of public teachers and preachers of the Word. When the total cessation of miracles ensued, they had, in dependence on heaven's blessing to look to their gymnasia and academies for fresh supplies. These were, in fact, the grand substitute for miracles, under the subsequent ordinary dispensation of Providence. And from the close of the apostolic age downwards, whence came almost all public teachers?—Whence but from the ancient schools? Whence came the great body of the reformers—the men most honoured of God in their evangelistic labours, next to the apostles themselves?—Whence but from the schools and seminaries, established in different parts of Europe? Whence do the Christian churches and Missionary Societies at present derive supplies, whether for the home or the foreign field?—Whence but from the very same sources? And whence can we expect to receive the thousands of qualified natives who shall overtake the realms of heathenism? Only from similar sources opened up, and bountifully replenished in every land!

The *third* and *last* of the great measures of evangelization, is the TRANSLATION AND CIRCULATION OF THE SACRED SCRIPTURES. Connected with the prosecution of this object, there are as many broad fallacies, as many crude and undigested notions afloat, as on the subject of education and preaching. It is not a little curious that, among the most enthusiastic advocates of Bible and Tract circulation, are to be found many who are the most hostile to education—as if the distributed Bible could be of any avail to a people without an antecedent education to qualify them for perusing it!—that very education without which we might as well send harps to the deaf, or paintings to the blind, as disperse Bibles among any people wholly destitute of it! But letting that pass,—when once a translation is completed in the language of any province, how common, how very general the exclamation, "The Word of God is now thrown open to so many millions!" When translations in whole, or in part, have been made into all the leading languages and dialects of a country like India, how frequent the remark, "The Word of God is now thrown open to nearly the whole of its inhabitants!" From all this, the tacit inference often is, that the word of life must be virtually, if not actually, scattered like spiritual seed, and diffused like spiritual leaven over all the Indian continent—and that from this source alone, a prodigious harvest of quickened and ripened fruit is about to be reaped!

Is there not a grand fallacy involved in such large expectations? Think of a country suffering from universal famine,—to the famine has succeeded universal pestilence. The government opens granaries of wholesome provision in central spots. You then exclaim,—"Behold a redundant store of nutriment thrown open to the whole empire!" But what a mockery of benevolence were this, when all are so diseased that they have no relish, no desire for food,—when the reception of food might only nurse them the more rapidly for the grave? Well, side by side, you next establish a magazine of restorative medicaments; and you now exclaim,—"Behold a copious, an overflowing store of balsamic remedies is thrown open to the whole land!" Of what avail is this, if almost all the population are so debilitated and stupified with disease that they are either unable or unwilling to come and receive the necessary supplies? Well, you then send quantities of healing drugs indiscriminately to every door. But,—there being no kind friend to ply the insensible patient,—no skilful physician to administer these drugs according to the phases of the distemper, modified endlessly by peculiarities of constitution, and previous dietetic and professional habits,—they are wholly overlooked or rejected by the majority. Portions swallowed at random by others, either effect no good or prove positively injurious,—being speedily assimilated with the circulating fluids, or transmuted into venom that feeds and inflames the malady. And would it materially rescue the scheme from the charge of ineffi-

one in whose expanded and sanctified intellect, in whose enlarged and purified heart, the seed of all quickening truth, human and divine, has been implanted. There it takes root and germinates. Fraught with vivifying power, up it springs into a stately stem of intelligence and godliness;—outward it shoots its vigorous branches, laden with the sap of grace and fructifying knowledge; and these again cast down their fibres of instruction and living influence, which fasten in the soil of other heads and other hearts. Thence arises many a new stem of fruitful piety, which, by a similar process, extends outwards,—again descends and springs up;—and so onwards without end,—till the whole land be converted into a beauteous garden, replenished with "plants of renown"—plants of righteousness—which, though endowed with their own several individual identities, are yet so many inseparably united members of the great tree of life, whose leaves are for the healing of the nations.

Hitherto, in the magnificence of empire, India has been truly said to have found nothing more precious, either to possess or be proud of possessing, than—

> " Fiery opals, sapphires, amethysts,
> Jacinths, hard topaz, grass-green emeralds,
> Beauteous rubies, sparkling diamonds,
> And seld-seen costly stones of so great price,
> As one of them, indifferently rated,
> May serve, in peril of calamity,
> To ransom great kings from captivity."

Happy day for India!—when, through the descent of the Spirit's influences on the devoted labours of her own emancipated sons, the garden of her early youth which has so long been parched into utter barrenness, shall be made verdant and fruitful by the distilling dews of heavenly instruction;—and the vale of her riper years, which has so long been strewn with nought but forms, cold and lifeless as the dry bones in the valley of vision, shall be enlivened by the trumpet peals of the Gospel message, and the stirring activities of a resurrection from the dead;—and the channels of all her knowledge, which have so long been choked into stagnation by every thing noxious and venomous, shall be cleansed by letting in upon them a full stream from the fount itself of living waters, in God's holy oracles. Then will India, even in the magnificence of empire, find no costly stone half so precious as the new jewel that hath been put into her hands —even the jewel of great price which hath ransomed, not only great kings, but great kingdoms, from their captivity,—aye, and the whole creation itself from the bondage, under which for ages it hath travailed and groaned. Then will India, even in the magnificence of empire, find no "clothing of wrought gold," no "raiment of needle-work," half so royal as the new robes wherewith she hath been clad,—robes woven of the beams of the Sun of Righteousness. Then will India, even in the magnificence of empire, find no delight in the possession of her "fiery opals and beauteous rubies, her grass-green emeralds and sparkling diamonds," half so great as her abounding joy in casting these down, as tributes of homage and free-will offerings of gratitude, at the feet of her long despised but now adored Immanuel.

Note.—After the preceding chapter was wholly written and sent to the press, the author was favoured with the perusal of an able work, by an eminently calm and dispassionate observer, as well as zealous and distinguished friend of missions—the Rev. Mr Malcolm; who was recently sent to South Eastern Asia, on a missionary tour of inspection, by one of the great American Societies. In that work, many of the views contained in the chapter now closed, are not only substantially corroborated, but some of them expressed in terms fully more strong than the author had deemed it advisable to adopt. In the section relative to "*the disadvantages under which the best and purest missionary labour is exerted*," Vol. II. p. 265, Mr Malcolm enumerates, amongst others, the following particulars.

1. An imperfect knowledge of the language of the people.

"Scarcely one missionary in twenty has become able to preach with entire fluency, and probably never one had such a knowledge of the language as inspiration gave. Few can acquire such mastery of a foreign tongue, as to express their thoughts with the glow and intensity of a native, even when the idiom and structure of the language is thoroughly understood.

"An experienced missionary in Bengal assured me, that on an average, not one half of the sermons of missionaries who undertake to preach is understood. Dr Carey, in a letter of August, 1809, states that after, by years of study, he thought he had fully mastered the Bengali, and had then preached it two full years, he discovered that he was not understood! Yet Dr C.'s teachers flattered him that he was understood perfectly. This is a very common deception of pandits and munshis. In the opinion of one of

Priscilla Chapman

Hindoo Female Education. London: R.B. Seeley ad W. Burnside, 1839.

CHAPTER VII.

NECESSITY OF A PRINCIPLE THAT WILL ESTABLISH MUTUAL CONFIDENCE—ENGLISH EDUCATION—EXCLUSION OF SCRIPTURE FROM GOVERNMENT SCHOOLS—COMPARATIVE INFLUENCE OF MISSIONARY LABOR—NATIVE CO-OPERATION NOT TO BE EXPECTED—DIFFICULTIES OF FINDING RIGHTLY QUALIFIED TEACHERS IN INDIA—PROGRESS HITHERTO LIMITED TO THE POOR—MEANS OF EXTENSION.

It is the practice in questions of European polity, to contemplate the constitution of society, with reference to certain acknowledged rights, admitted to be inherent in ourselves; and a renovating principle is appealed to, the powers of which, for whatever period they may have been dormant, are never supposed to have ceased entirely: on the contrary, when circumstances call them into action, they often appear to have gathered fresh vigour from the occasion of repose.

No such self-regulating compact is to be found amongst the Hindoos, either in civil or domestic society; which is the great reason for their disunion and consequent weakness: the tyranny of caste has expunged any record of the civil rights of man, whilst custom and prejudice have taken the place of law and principle. It is a distinguishing feature of their system, that they must continue in the position of their progenitors, whether good or bad: thus occupations and habits are never changed, but descend from generation to generation. The greatest evil is endured in preference to, what they consider, the slightest innovation of old customs; and in no instance is this more apparent, than in the home circle, where discord, confusion, and misery reign, from the long-established idea, that the wife must and ought to be the slave, instead of the help-meet. There is one exception, however, which we would mention, as in itself worthy of admiration, though sometimes evil in its consequences: the attachment which the Hindoo feels to the inheritance of his fathers; for, like the vineyard of Naboth the Jezreelite, it is neither the better land or the worth of it in money, that would readily induce the exchange, so that property often lies waste and useless, in the hands of its proprietor, which would otherwise become valuable.

It is quite essential for the right direction of measures intended to benefit the people, that the real character of their feelings and customs, should be understood, and that fear of consequences should never induce even apparent respect for what is evil. The Hindoo knows how to value consistency in others, though he has no courage to maintain it in his own conduct; and it is not indulgence to their prejudices, that gives power over them. No compromise with Hindooism or Mahomedanism, will ever succeed in gaining that influence which will do the people real good. A completely new principle of feeling and action must be given. There are many indeed amongst the Hindoos, and even the Brahmins, who venture to prognosticate, that a new era will soon commence, when their nation will become Christian. But it is not well to indulge here in these deep and interesting anticipations; present duties are sufficiently momentous.

The readiness with which all classes have accepted the national boon of English education, Hindoo and Mussulman attending the same college, shows both a zeal and capability for receiving such knowledge, as may qualify them for employment under government; but shackled as the instruction is, by obligations to which the authorities hold themselves bound, *not to interfere with their religious opinions*, they may alas! 'be ever learning, and never able to come to the knowledge of the truth.'

Encouragement of a much more pleasing character is to be derived from the attendance at the missionary schools, where the whole instruction rests upon divine truth. In all the Female and Missionary Boys' schools, the object of giving Christian instruction is avowed in the most open manner, and it is altogether impossible for those who send their children to such institutions, not to know that they are instructed in the Christian religion, and invited to embrace the hopes and promises, as well as confident assurances of the pardoning mercy of God, which are presented to the sinful children of men in the gospel of his son. In the avowed purpose of government to exclude the Scriptures and religious books even from the libraries, the Church and the individual Christian may be said to possess a charter in their favor; though it is seldom indeed that real conversion takes place whilst the children remain in the schools, they being minors till the age of sixteen; yet the difference of moral effect under the two systems is very apparent.

With reference to female education, it is impossible for government to interfere; neither can the means for improving the condition of the female population become the subject of legislation. This makes it important that other means should be discovered, to assist and benefit them. It would be vain to encourage a hope of the Brahmins' assenting, and becoming instrumental in the education of the sex so degraded. They never can act in concert in any matter which has not the immediate tendency to enrich themselves; and were they so disposed, it must be borne in mind, that their influence would work additional misery, by exposing the female character still more prominently to the influence of the religion of Kali, which is justly designated, 'pure unmixed evil.' Not merely is the absence of confidence in native society a bar to all advancement, but the "fear of man" is exemplified in the Hindoo character to an inconceivable extent, and paralyses the best powers. It is next to an impossibility to obtain the united attention of natives, even in immediate association with Europeans, for any subject of improvement, though they generally admit its probable advantage, without hesitation. Fair promises of consultation with others are always given, but they seldom, amount to any thing further; for no one has the courage to be *the first to begin any thing new.* We must not therefore indulge any expectation of measures promoting the female welfare, being originated, or finding ready support from the Hindoos themselves.

Hitherto the East Indian population, descendants of Europeans in India, have had little or no weight with the natives: there are but few subjects of interest calculated to bring their united energies into action, and as an independent community, they are very deficient in those characteristics which qualify for the exercise of influence; if we except their familiar acquaintance with the vernacular language, an attainment which the European acquires with considerable difficulty, and probably never with the same fluency of expression. At Madras, the Rev. C. Tucker has made an important effort to give to the education of the East Indian females, such a direction as may bring valuable assistance to the work; and we trust that the day is not far distant, when many will be so established and settled in the faith, as to give them an influence, beyond that of mere tuition, with the Hindoos. Of the orphan children of European parents, educated in charitable institutions in India, from whom assistance might have been reasonably expected, but few have hitherto become serviceable in this sphere; there is every inducement for these young women to marry early, and a proper fear of associating with the heathen, has degenerated into a prejudice, that any contact with the natives is degrading. An encouraging example has been shown by such as have come forward, and the hope must be indulged, that the education which they receive, may be blessed in qualifying and disposing them to engage in this important service. The time is not yet arrived, that we can look to the converts to Christianity for any independent efforts; the sufferings which attend the sincere and faithful avowal of the truth, are such as leave them frequently in a state of great weakness, and they themselves are the objects of their pastor's unceasing prayerful attention. Some years must elapse, before children of Christian converts now under instruction, can be fitted, if ever they should be disposed, to engage in duties of charity, towards their benighted countrywomen.

For the reasons thus stated, it seems not only necessary, but natural to look to Christian countries, and especially to England, to supply the means that are required for the instruction of the Hindoos or Mahomedan females. It is clear that native females of good caste need but little encouragement to dispose them to welcome ladies who would visit them with a Christian object: none but such as are experienced in their Christian course can, under existing circumstances, hazard the attempt; and it is equally true, that when not merely the jealous character of the men must be overcome, but if possible, their confidence secured, the character and deportment of the visiting lady should be such as is calculated to command respect.

The 'Ladies' Society' in Calcutta, in the hope

that their countrywomen will not turn a deaf ear to so strong an appeal, have made known their readiness to provide visiting teachers, whenever they may be called for. We cannot however forget that we are taught in the gospel, "that not many wise men after the flesh, not many mighty, not many noble are called: but God hath chosen the foolish things of the world to confound the wise: and God hath chosen the weak things of the world to confound the things which are mighty; and base things of the world, and things which are despised hath God chosen: yea, and things which are not to bring to nought things that are." The dissemination of the Gospel in India is no exception, and in the humble efforts hitherto made for the female population, it is almost exclusively to the poor, that the glad tidings have been carried. That they have not been wholly unwilling hearers, will be evinced by facts, and those who have seen the children under Christian tuition, are struck with the effect of the benefit conferred, legible in their countenances: nor can it be doubted that the marked distinction between the expression of unmeaning vacancy, and that given by a mind occupied with good thoughts, must be more or less perceptible to the parents, to whom the richest blessings may thus be conveyed through the weakest instrumentality.

Though the actual improvement of character is apparently small, under the tuition which has been given; yet when the children of the lower castes that have been instructed in any of the female schools, are compared with those of the highest rank, the contrast in mind and manner is strikingly in favour of the former.

The effect of European influence upon native society, is however far from being a subject of exultation: for when it is remembered what is the power of example upon the heathen, every one must feel a deep humiliation, and confess that the profession of Christianity in India has hitherto been very unproductive. As a nation, we are progressively brought into a nearer connexion with the millions of our fellow-subjects in India, and their welfare should not merely be the concern of residents in the east, who have many claims upon them; but occupy the prayerful and constant endeavours of the church at large.

In a work of this character, the disproportion of time and means to the magnitude of the undertaking, would be altogether an overwhelming discouragement, unless it be viewed in the light of a direct fulfilment of the commandment of our Lord. To the minds of such as think that happiness can exist where the gospel is unknown, and that the Hindoo, being enlightened by useful knowledge alone, will care for the moral and intellectual condition of their females, no expectation of carrying conviction can be entertained; but such persons are entreated to search still closer into the subject, with the sincere desire that infinite wisdom may teach them to distinguish between truth and error.

Irene Barnes

Between Life and Death: The Story of C.E.Z.M.S. Medical Missions in India, China, and Ceylon, London: Marshall Brothers, 1901.

CHAPTER VI

CLINICAL CHRISTIANITY.

or

Hospitals and Dispensaries in North India and Bengal.

"The spirit of Missions is the spirit of sympathy, of self denial and of service, which is only another way of saying that it is the spirit of Christ."—*J. C. Smith, D.D.*

"I believe, notwithstanding all that the English people have done to benefit India, the missionaries have done more than all other agencies combined."—*Lord Lawrence.*

IT is our purpose in the following chapters to depict as far as may be the principal homes of healing founded by the C.E.Z.M.S. While the details differ, and the pictures are of varying light and shade, the one aim is prominent through all: to bring sin-sick souls in contact with Christ, the Great Physician.

Medical Mission work is attempted in nearly every station in the foreign field occupied by this Society: but it may not be generally known how great a work on these lines has sprung up of recent years and how increasingly the Society individually and collectively recognizes that Medical Missionary work in its true form, viz., as carried on by fully equipped physicians, is becoming an absolutely necessary adjunct to, or rather integral part of. each Mission Station.

The Society to-day (1901) has no fewer than

fifteen hospitals, situated in Amritsar, Krishnagar, Ratnapur, Baharwal-Atari, Batala, Ajnala, Jandiala, Narowal, Tarn-Taran, Peshawar, Quetta, Bangalore, Trevandrum, Foochow and Lo-Nguong : each with its accompanying out-patient department; and Dispensaries also (without Hospitals) in Calcutta, Mankar, Dera Ismail Khan, Hyderabad, Sukkur, Srinagar, Khammamett, Gampola, Dang Seng, and Kucheng; also the care of a ward in the Native Hospital, Foochow.

Eight of these stations are in the charge of European fully-qualified lady doctors. Six are in the care of ladies who have had a two years' medical course of training in England. Four are placed under those who have had from two to four years' training at St. Catherine's, Amritsar, and the remaining workers in charge have had shorter periods of medical study.

We are well aware that only such Medical Missions as are worked by fully-qualified members of the medical profession are strictly entitled to be thus called. Yet for obvious reasons we venture to include a description of work which, in however small a measure, combines healing with preaching the Gospel under our sketches of Medical Mission agency.

It was in answer to many prayers that a fully-qualified lady doctor offered her generous help for the women of the Mahommedan Mission, Calcutta. Mrs. Mills, L.R.C.P. & S., Ed., had only just arrived from England (1900), and, owing to her marriage, was no longer practising. The over-pressed workers, longing for a fellow-helper with the skill so much needed, welcomed her aid with intense thankfulness.

Funds came in to keep open the tiny dispensary opened by Mis Bardsley, and to support a trained assistant from St. Catherine's, Amritsar, for a year. At first the girls' schoolroom was used in lieu of a better place; then the missionaries' own abode was invaded, and a small mud room belonging to the mission house was rented. But after several weeks, finding themselves packed into it with eighty patients and a temperature over 100°, they were obliged to hire a second room, and now (1901) a third small mud hut is to be rented.

The Dispensary is open two days a week, and is besieged with grateful patients, as many as fifty attending in one day. More would come if they could, but the majority are so poor that to hire a *duli* is almost an impossibility. Their bigotry melts away into gratitude to their benefactors, and attention to the Message which the Bible-woman faithfully proclaims. The busy mother is away from the distractions of her Zenana, and her heart softens and gives heed to the things spoken.

It is hoped shortly to start a second small Dispensary at another Mahommedan centre—Tallygunge. But again, here, the cry of the workers is for a fully-qualified doctor and Zenana Hospital, which ought to be in every Mission centre.

The life of a missionary in the midst of heathen villages is an illustration of the days when the Good Physician was thronged by suffering multitudes until there was "no leisure so much as to eat." Out in the vast Nuddea district of Bengal numbers of sick have had to be sent away in the days before a Mission Dispensary was established and a doctor was sent out. Yet the elementary knowledge possessed by the Missionary-in-Charge, Miss Dawe, made her famous, although she refused to undertake any serious case, and sick people travelled three days' journeys to place themselves under her care. A large proportion of the patients were suffering from skin diseases and ordinary fevers, and the chief remedies for these were cleanliness, care, and common sense, cures all easily procurable indeed, yet needing to be instilled into the Bengali women's mind. It is marvellous to see how they will carefully bind up a wound with the filthiest of rags; and where burning fever is consuming the strength of a loved child, the mother believes she is doing wisely by withholding every kind of nourishment.

Thus a medical branch of the Village Mission grew up of itself, without intention on the part of those who began the work—Miss Dawe and her one helper, the faithful Bible-woman, Rachel.

"My first peep at the work, in 1891," says Miss F. C. Brown, "was to find Miss Dawe sitting on the verandah of a mud house in which she had been holding a meeting, surrounded by an eager group of women, each with a bottle or vessel of some sort, while medicinal directions were being carefully given. The medicine were carried about by the Missionary in a rough wooden box made by a village carpenter easily conveyable by *tum-tum*. In 1892, a friend in England sent out as her representative a worker whom a short Hospital training in England rendered able and eager to help in the medical work, and soon after Miss Owles had joined the Mission, a small Dispensary was opened in a *go-down* that had been fitted up with shelves and a supply of medicines. At once the number of women and children out-patients doubled, even though a fee of two *pice* was charged, so as to ensure that only those needing medicine themselves would apply.

So many wounds and sores were healed, so many fevers cured, that the Miss *Sahiba's* fame spread all over the district and the numbers grew. The headquarters were now removed from Bollobhpur to Ratnapur, and Miss Trench joined the staff, having studied medicine and Indian diseases at St. Catherine's Hospital, Amritsar. A mud house was dignified by the name of temporary Hospital, though in reality it was only a shelter in which a patient might stay a few days, their relatives making all arrangements for cooking, &c.

The extent of the work by this time is seen from the fact that in one year, 38,000 out-patients, coming from 900 different villages, were treated: while the immensely wide seed-scattering which took place will be realized when it is known that each patient received a very simple Gospel tract, printed in Bengali on the back of her prescription. This paper containing particulars of treatment, &c., was to be carefully produced on each visit to the Dispensary. A translation of the tract runs as follows:—

"Why have you come to the Dispensary? Is it not because you are sick and wish to get well? You believe that if the Doctor Miss *Sahiba* gives you medicine you are sure to get well. How she will heal you, you do not know, but you believe she wishes to, and will do all in her power for it. The Doctor Miss *Sahiba* cannot heal all the sick nor drive away every disease. She is not God, but only human, but she tries to make the sick ones well, and often does so, and her medicines act on the diseases. But besides this there is another kind of disease far worse than that of the body. We call it the disease of the soul. Whether rich or poor, whether young or old, whether male or female, all have this disease. What is it, and who can heal it?

"This disease is sin! There is no one who has not sinned. Are *you* without sin? The Doctor Miss *Sahiba* cannot heal this disease, but she knows who can. There is only One in the world who can heal this soul-disease. He is Jesus, the Son of God. *Jesus can put away all sin and heal everyone;* for He is God. It is written in the Gospel, 'All power is given unto Me in heaven and in earth.'

"*Jesus wishes to heal everyone.* He says, 'Come unto Me, all ye that are weary and heavy-laden and I will give you rest.' Also, 'God so loved.' &c. (St. Jno. iii. 16).

"*Jesus has promised to heal.* He says, 'Him that cometh to Me I will in no wise cast out.' Do you wish to be healed from the disease of sin? Do you wish for a new and clean heart? Come to Jesus: He will heal you. Great or small, all who have come to Him have been healed, every one.

"At the Dispensary each morning something will be

told you about this. Listen attentively, and you will find out how you can come to Jesus and be healed."

Funds for building a Hospital were sent in answer to prayer, and were placed in Miss Dawe's and Miss Trench's hands when on furlough in England, and the still more valuable acquisition, a fully qualified lady doctor, Miss V. Von Himpé, M.D., was provided who took over the entire charge of the medical work in June, 1897. Miss E. Owles, with true self-effacement, wrote thus of the event: "None gave a heartier welcome to her rightful post than the 'quacks' who now gladly hide their diminished heads for ever and a day."

The new building was opened with much thanksgiving and prayer on New Year's Day, 1900, by the Rev. F. Paynter, whose munificent donation to the building fund had made its erection possible.

All the C.M.S. pastors, teachers, Bible women, and Church members from the neighbouring Christian villages were invited to the opening ceremony, which took place under the fine, stately trees in the compound. The Clergy, the Rev. E. T. Butler and the Rev. Koilash C. Day, conducted an impressive little service, Bengali-English forming equal parts in the proceedings. After the benediction had been pronounced, Dr. Von Himpe presented Mr. Paynter with the key of the Hospital, who, having unlocked the door, declared the building opened and stated the motive and object of its work in a few appropriate sentences.

The Hospital, in reality one large ward, has been fitted up with great completeness of appointments for the care of the sick. The Dispensary, a twin building, is in a prominent position quite close to the road. It consists of four rooms, for dispensing, consulting, dressing, and stores, and has a verandah to accommodate the patients.

During one year as many as twenty-seven in-patients have been received, and nearly 9,000 have visited the Dispensary.

Dr. Von Himpé has also opened a Dispensary made of mud and thatched with straw at Meherpur, a small town about eight miles from Ratnapur. The itinerating doctor finds her bicycle an invaluable steed in the cold, dry weather. She says: "The little cow-boys are delighted to see the Miss *Sahiba* coming. They shout at the top of their voices and try to keep up with her as long as possible. Meeting a herd of cows is a funny experience. Buffaloes, too, take to

The Dispensary at Meherpur, Nuddea, Bengal.

their heels and flee for their lives from the uncanny machine, and it is most ridiculous to see those bulky creatures running."

The *tum-tum* is, however, the more usual mode of conveyance, as it can hold a Bible woman and *tiffin* basket: but sometimes during the rainy season, the river is the only road left, and then several long hours must be spent in the Mission boat.

Several *bows* in the town have invited the doctor to see

and prescribe for them and give, not only her, but her Message a warmly appreciative reception. Often their neighbours are invited and so quite a small congregation is assembled. The work in this out-station is growing amazingly, and now (1901) the Missionary physician has an ever-increasing number of patients awaiting her at the Dispensary and many more eager requests to visit the higher caste women in their own homes.

Kushtia, a small town in the N.E. of the Nuddea district, has recently become another permanent out-station and point of Medical Mission interest. A Dispensary was opened in 1899, and Mrs. Peters, a certificated nurse and Bible woman, has been successfully prosecuting very real Medical Mission work in the homes of the people. Miss C. P. Marks, who has been in charge of the Dispensary for a time, speaks of the gratitude of the women for relief.

"Some fall down on the ground to touch our feet with their foreheads, saying how good the medicine was and how much better they are. Others bring as a thank-offering some minute fish in a particularly dirty piece of cloth. Of course the cloth is dirty. Who would think of putting fish into a clean cloth? Others again bring eggs and native fruit. Though we are generally glad to hand over these dainties to the Bible-women, it is always a source of joy to know the feeling which prompted the gifts."

Miss C. Harding.

Although not yet entitled to the name of Medical Mission, simple remedies to the suffering folk of Mankar, in the Burdwan district, have been administered so freely and with such remarkable results by our Missionary in charge of the station as to call for very special mention.

The work virtually began in 1898, when Miss C. Harding, on her itinerating tour in the cool weather, took with her a small stock of medicines, having previously found herself besieged for medical advice from those to whom an English lady and *sinyana* or wise woman are synonymous terms.

In those villages visited before she had a warm welcome, and now the news quickly spread, that 'the *Mem* who gives the medicine has come.' Forthwith the halt, maimed, and blind were brought and placed before her, in the firm expectation that something could be done at once for them, no matter how complicated the diseases might be.

Often Miss Harding and her companion, Miss M. Lloyd, would find a crowd awaiting them on returning from a village to their breakfast. This meal they would have to partake of in the midst of a group of watching "patients" who would spring forward the moment the repast was finished, each wishing to be the first served. Only very simple physic was dispensed, neither of our Missionaries professing to be doctors: but God wonderfully blessed the remedies, and made them a lever to raise the barrier of prejudice and open hearts to the Gospel.

Soon after the workers opened a small Dispensary at their village Mission centre at Mankar, twenty miles north of Burdwan; and a trained medical student from St. Catherine's Hospital was appointed to assist them. Immediately the news spread and patients came from twenty miles away. Numbers of villages never before visited were thus reached, for day by day the Gospel was lovingly proclaimed to the waiting women. In five months no fewer than 1,460 patients attended the Dispensary, coming from as many as sixty-two villages and thirty *parahs* (Hindu or Moslem quarters) of Mankar district.

Such a work had to go though a baptism of fire; and a month after the opening of this place of healing a memorable disturbance was wrought by the Enemy of Souls, whose territory was being so powerfully invaded.

A little, famine-stricken child was brought to our Missionaries. The child's mother died on the road from starvation, and left her little boy and girl, ten and seven years of age, in the hands of a poor woman travelling in the same company. This woman came to the Dispensary for medicine, bringing with her the little waif. Poor wee mite, she was quite willing to stay and be fed, but her little brother raised a hue and

Mankar Mission House.

The Dispensary is at the right-hand corner; the Verandah in front is used as Dressing Room. Patients sit under the porch to the right.

cry, and one hundred men, armed with sticks, mobbed the house, and demanded the child. Being of the lowest caste, they did not really want her, but merely came to annoy the ladies, because they were jealous of their influence, and of the friendliness of the people.

We continue in the words of our heroic workers :— "We shall never forget that eventful day! We defenceless women faced an infuriated mob of the worst characters in the place. The ringleader was a man who sells drink, and he urged the people to strike us down if we would not give up the child. He offered one hundred rupees to the man who would so injure me that I should never be able to preach the Gospel again. Their shrieks of "Beat the *Mem*," "Bring out the child," "Tear down the house," "Disgrace the *Mems*," were deafening. It was in vain that we tried to explain why we had shown kindness to the child. One man held his fists so close to my face that I expected a blow every moment. Then the words came to me as if audibly spoken, 'Fear not, I am with thee.' God did indeed stand by me, and held back the hands of those men, who seemed, for the time, possessed by Satan."

In the end, much to the grief of our ladies, the child had to be given up, although the case was tried in the Indian law court, that so better protection might be afforded to the Missionaries. The prayers of Christians at home were fully answered and the people became more friendly than ever. Not a stone was thrown, not an insulting word was said, as the workers went in and out among them as usual. But the greatest astonishment was displayed at the ladies' courage, and the people wondered how it was that "*women* should have the power of kings."

A remarkable sequel followed. Some months afterwards Miss Harding was called at the eleventh hour to see a little child very ill with fever, who had been treated with blisters, &c., by two heavily-feed native quacks. Entirely in answer to prayer, God blessed the remedies used, to the child's complete recovery, and a great impression was made on the family. Shortly after, the wife asked for medicine for her husband, who was suffering from a bad cough. Imagine the surprise of our Missionary when, at her next visit, the master of the house prostrated himself in grateful homage at her feet, and when face to face with him, she recognized the foremost rioter on that eventful day, who had stood over her with his club, threatening her life if she did not give up the famine waif!

The man's heart was completely softened. Each time, thenceforth, that the Missionary went in and out of his house she was welcomed as a friend, and her Message was received.

Thus does "Clinical Christianity" appeal to the hearts and consciences of the people of Mankar. In hostile villages, where, formerly, 1,000 rupees were set

Interior of the Dispensary, Mission House, Mankar.

on the Missionary's head, and where the workers had fearlessly continued visiting and giving simple remedies during a visitation of cholera, they now receive the warmest welcome.

New patients continue to come to the Dispensary, being advised by their friends to "go to the *Mems* who give good medicine without price, and speak kind, holy words," and medicine is still taken on itinerating tours. Two workers will sit by the roadside, on the highway to a market town, and, with their medicines arranged before them, waylay the passers-by. Nearly a hundred people will thus hear the Gospel and receive some remedy in a single morning. On one occasion, a man was beginning to argue on behalf of his gods, when another bystander called out, "Did the gods ever put it into the heart of anyone of our doctors to give medicine for nothing, as the *mem* is doing?"

Even in the forest villages a welcome awaits their *didi*, or elder sister, as the women delight to call their Missionary friend. "*Didi* has come and brought her medicines, and she speaks good words; come and listen."

The Dispensary is held in the little house occupied by the Missionaries. The patients begin to assemble at 7 a.m., and, before they are attended to, prayers are held in the dining-room with the Bible women. Naturally, the women are inquisitive enough to pull aside the curtain to discover what the *Mems* are doing, and the remark of one patient to another is often overheard, "These Christians pray to God to bless the medicine, and that is why it does us so much good."

"They have wonderful faith in us," says Miss Harding, "and, though we tell them we are not doctors—I often wish I were a doctor, and need send none away!—they are certain we can do something. 'What! all those medicines and you cannot give me one drop!' said an old woman who had walked twenty miles, when I told her I could do nothing for her disease because I am not a doctor. We are sorely needing a fully-equipped medical lady, and are asking God to send us one."

At Mankar, our Missionaries are twenty-five miles from a doctor; and there is no Medical Mission throughout the Burdwan district—somewhat larger than Lancashire, and containing one million and a half of inhabitants.

Krishnagar, a sacred Hindu city, the resort of

pilgrims to the shrine of Chaitanya, is a stronghold of Hinduism, and, therefore, has its own special difficulties as a Mission Station. Here, in consequence, Medical Mission work became slowly, but surely indispensable to the success of the general agency. Opposition amounting almost to persecution attended the earliest efforts, but prejudice was overcome, and through the kindness chiefly of the former Collector and his wife, the workers were able to build and double the size of the original Dispensary.

Miss R. M. Phailbus has had charge of the Medical work ever since it began in 1890, and is now assisted by Miss Bose. Miss Phailbus is a Panjabi lady, who had five years' medical training at St. Catherine's, Amritsar, and holds Government diplomas. In her one sees a remarkably encouraging specimen of the result of Missionary effort. Her father was a native clergyman, she was educated in the Alexandra High School, was trained at a Mission Hospital, and is now labouring as a Medical Missionary among her Indian sisters, respected and loved by all with whom she has to do. She is assisted by a staff of Bengali trained assistants. The Dispensary is situated in the middle of the town, and in a very bigoted portion of it. The verandah, holding about eighty patients, is packed with women every morning except Saturday and Sunday, and singing of Gospel hymns, and preaching goes on every day for about four hours. As many as 1,900 new patients, and 1,300 old patients will receive treatment at the Dispensary, and seven hundred visits at least will be paid to others at their homes during the year.

One day a woman appeared and informed Miss Phailbus that she had walked twelve miles as she had heard that the Missionary knew how to feel pulses. She looked plump and well, so she was asked why she wanted her pulse felt. "To know when I am going to die," she replied, to the amusement of the other patients. But advantage was taken of the incident to point this dark soul to Christ, and she went away much impressed.

No charge is made for medicine, but the patients have to bring their own "bottles," and it is amusing to see the extraordinary variety of receptacles covered by that word. A woman will present a tiny bottle expecting that a cough mixture to last two days for her child, and a lotion for her own rheumatism can be put together, and is quite astonished when told to bring another and a larger bottle. They have become accustomed to taking medicine from Christians, although to take food from them would break caste: but even now, the water necessary for mixing the physic has to be kept in large medicine bottles, and dispensed like medicine to prevent arousing caste prejudices.

The Dispensary gate, opened at 7 a.m., is closed at 10.30 a.m.; but during that time, in the rainy season, as many as 200 patients will have entered. Each one receives and retains a numbered ticket for which she pays 2 *pice* on her first visit. These tickets are made from Mrs. Grimké's text-cards, and are often kept for years. The patients are passed into the consulting-room in order according to the numbers on their tickets.

A very interesting out-patient was a woman, Kamini by name, a silversmith's wife. For three months she came regularly to the Dispensary, bringing her little granddaughter with a bad foot, and would sit near the Bible-woman listening attentively. When the child recovered she returned to her home in a distant country town, taking a Gospel with her. Nearly two years afterwards, when a Zenana Missionary and this same Bible woman were out in camp, they came upon Kamini in her own home. It was touching to see the delight with which she welcomed them, and heard once more the Words of

Life. They found, to their great joy, that she was still believing in Christ, and speaking of Him to her children and Hindu neighbours.

For a long time the workers felt the need of, at least, a room where serious cases could be nursed for a time; and in the summer of 1895 they opened a tiny Hospital in their own compound. This was accomplished by fitting up the large "Converts' Room" as a ward, with portions separated at either end by wooden screens, to form a class room, doctor's examination room, and bathing (cemented) room for the patients.

It was no easy task for the superintending Missionary to oversee the carpentering required to make the screens fit into one another, and also into the uneven ground. All the wood-work that touched the floor had to be covered with pitch, to prevent the whole being eaten up by white ants. These uninvited inmates came up out of the ground in all directions—like an army. "I poured pitch into some of their habitations," said Miss Collisson, "only to see them come up out of a fresh hole. Then I bathed them in kerosine oil with better success."

The room, however, made a charming little extemporized Hospital. It contains six beds and a cot, and looks very airy and inviting, with bright Scripture pictures and texts hung around. It is very keenly appreciated. One of the beds, it is delightful to note, is being supported by the girls of a Mission School in China.

The iron beds and bedding are of the simplest description—straw mattresses laid on boards, two sheets and a counterpane, complete the furniture of each.

Patients are generally astir by 5.30 a.m. when the night nurse makes their beds. At 6 a.m. a Bible Class is held for the nurses every day except Saturday, the Hospital being left in the charge of a special helper.

After this the day nurse comes on duty, taking temperatures, giving out the milk and bread, and then undertaking all sponging and dressing of patients, which goes on until 10 o'clock. At 10.30 breakfast is given, some enjoying vegetables with curry and rice, and others sago and milk. Miss Phailbus usually makes her morning round at 7.30 a.m., and again at 12.30 midday. At 2 p.m., milk and soup and bread are served and then the patients have a quiet rest until 3.30, when the afternoon nurse comes to take the temperatures and to do other necessary things. At 5 o'clock the doctor again goes round and prescriptions, &c. are written. From 4 to 5 p.m. the patients are allowed to receive visits from their friends. After this prayers are taken. First a hymn is sung, followed by a short Gospel address and the offering of a simple prayer, committing each patient to the Great Physician's care. Then comes dinner, the diet varying according to the illness of the patient, after which those who are able to walk are sent into the open air for a little stroll. At 7 p.m. the night nurse comes on duty, and at 10 o'clock Miss Phailbus makes her last round.

Sunday differs in many respects from the ordinary day. No sweeping or dusting that is not absolutely necessary is done. and all surgical dressings that can be left safely wait until Monday. The Gospel address is given at 3.30 p.m., and very often the nurses sing to the patients in the evening. The patients are quick to observe and appreciate the difference made by the Christians on their holy day. Not very long ago a poor woman reported to the doctor on Monday morning that she had been suffering great pain on Saturday night. When remonstrated with for not having mentioned it before, she replied, "Yesterday was Sunday, how could I disturb God's Day with my ailments!"

Some especially interesting cases from a doctor's point of view have been treated successfully in this small Home of Healing. A poor, thin woman, brought in a bullock-cart by her husband, was found in a burning fever, her right leg and knee a mass of running sores. She had been treated by all the village doctors and quacks, who had given her up as a hopeless case. The assistant surgeon at the Government Hospital had advised amputation, and for the first two months at Krishnagar, this last resource seemed inevitable. Ten weeks after her admission, her little baby was born, and soon afterwards she began to improve, though she was unable to leave her bed for four and a half months. When at last she left the Hospital, the leg was almost completely healed, and has proved to be permanently cured. It is not surprising that she believes that the Christians have a prayer-hearing God.

Although the patients shew a good deal of fortitude in bearing pain, they shrink from anything that can be likened to an operation. The sight of a clinical thermometer is quite enough to frighten many a woman, who will rush away screaming should she be requested to place such an "instrument" under her arm.

From the beginning of the work, there have been definite spiritual results. Some of the patients have become earnest Christian workers as teachers or assistant medical helpers. One, a Mahommedan, in spite of her relatives' opposition, was received into the Converts' Home at Baranagore, and was there baptized. Her life has been most consistent ever since. By her own desire she returned to the Mission House at Krishnagar to learn to be a nurse in the same Hospital and Dispensary where she herself found Christ.

The seven beds in this little Hospital are always full, and many cases have to be refused. The two workers and their staff have their hands full with the two dispensaries, the hospital, and private visiting. The visits of out-patients in the year now amount to nearly 27,000, and over 700 visits have been paid to pardah patients in the same period. The houses of the rich and high caste have alike opened to Zenana Missionaries through the successful medical treatment. Even the Palace was re-opened to Christian teaching through the same influence, the young Rani having received benefit from Miss Phailbus' medical advice, and thereafter giving her and her friend, the Zenana Missionary, a warm and loving welcome.

The Dispensary has now (1901) again to be enlarged, owing to the requirements of the steadily growing work. This has aroused the jealousy of the Hindus and much opposition, so that, for a time the workmen were not allowed to go on building, and, although the new verandah is finished and in use, the Municipality will not yet consent to steps being put up. But our workers are fully assured that while, in this fresh outbreak of antagonism, the early history of the Mission is being repeated, God's work will not be overturned, and that He will over-rule all to the extension of His Kingdom.

CHAPTER XI

NATIVE NURSES AND *NATIVE NURSES*

or

The Training of Native Women

"If Asia is to be won for Christ, it must be through Christian Asiatics."

ALL that we have said in earlier chapters has surely gone to prove that our Heathen and Mahommedan sisters have little or no idea of nursing one another in times of sickness. They lie untended between life and death for all that they can do for each other in the way of ministration; and the patient, on her hard mat in a close, foul-smelling room or out-house, will usually be expected to do every thing for herself, and to require little attention. One of the earliest duties of our Medical Missionaries is to try to instill into the women's minds some ideas of right treatment of the sick.

In our sketches of the various C.E.Z. Hospitals and Dispensaries, we have merely touched lightly upon that most promising branch of our agencies, the training of Native Nurses. In this closing chapter we will glance at it more fully.

Again and again reference has been made to the assistance which is being given to our Missionaries in India by young Indian women, than whom, where fully equipped, no better agents can be found, and who, possibly, in time will supersede many European workers in the field. Much larger spheres will be open to them, and their influence and conduct must tell more powerfully with their countrywomen than that of the foreigner. When Hindu and Mahommedan women can have constantly before them women of their own

On the River Min, Fuh-Kien, China.

nation who are leading Christ-like lives, they will know that it is Christianity which makes the difference.

But it must be remembered that this ideal state of things is still very far from being realized. A much longer, a more patient, as well as careful and strict training is necessary in order to make our Indian sisters as efficient as our own countrywomen. They inherit, as a rule, defects conspicuous in Oriental character which militate against accuracy, promptitude, and activity. They have inherent faults and failings to overcome which are as binding upon them as second nature. Order and method are not only unnatural to the Eastern mind, but are difficult to be appreciated by it. For example, a young native nurse-in-training will assert that she has given a patient her medicine if she puts the powder into her hand, although she knows perfectly well that it was thrown away and was not taken; and an older woman, a matron, will listen to the nurse's statement, and not correct it. Yet, by God's grace in the student's heart, and patient, firm training on the part of the European in charge, these faults can be and are being overcome. Not only are Indian women to-day efficient nurses, compounders, and druggists, but assistants and physicians, holding responsible positions, and carrying on successfully the work of two-fold healing among their countrywomen.

Continually it is demonstrated that Indian womanhood, under Christian influence, is able to be relied upon, not only for the routine work of the Hospital ward, but to meet the gravest emergencies. The saying is true, "It requires but the application of Christian truth to the heart, followed by thorough professional training, to make strong characters of any people."

If lady doctors are required, and competent nurses and dispensers to assist them, who can be so well fitted for the task as the women of the country? For they do not need to begin in mature life to grapple with a strange climate, an unknown language, and baffling social customs *plus* foreign modes of thought.

One of the oldest and most important training grounds for nurses is that at St. Catherine's Hospital, Amritsar. From that institution, young Indian medical evangelists have gone forth to be the right hand of many a Missionary in the field.*

As early as 1884, the training of medical students began to prove most successful. It was no small matter that of all the thousands of prescriptions made up, the ladies in charge of the work never had to dispense one themselves: also that all Hospital stores, linen, dressing, and other routine work was entirely taken off their hands. These pupils were trained in all the habits and ways of Missionary work and entered

*This School for Medical Students has ceased to exist, and nurses only are receiving training at St. Catherine's.

very enthusiastically into all efforts made to win and to teach the patients, taking their part in the Sunday School and in the daily reading and singing to in-patients, &c. Miss Hewlett wrote thus to friends at home in reference to this interesting and important development at St. Catherine's :—

A Lesson in Compounding.

"It cannot but be that native young ladies thus trained will find a very hearty welcome among their fellow-countrywomen, and we would ask the prayers of friends at home that their present and their future may be greatly blessed, and that they in their turn may train up others, and establish Dispensaries for the help and comfort of the women of India."

We have seen and are constantly witnessing how these prayers and anticipations have been abundantly fulfilled. Yet all the "raw material" sent in subsequent years to this training ground has not been of the finest calibre. In more than one case a girl was sent for training because "good for nothing else"; which expression, as Miss Hewlett dryly remarked, "so uncomplimentary to the noble profession of nursing would be rather trying for head lady nurses to hear, did they not know how very often 'good for nothingness' gets expelled by training and work." In 1900, a report could be given that several nurses had been passed on to work elsewhere, two of them being placed under Miss Basu, at Ajnala—Miss Basu herself having also been transferred from St. Catherine's early in the year.

The value of such trained women helpers to the European lady doctor cannot be exaggerated. No one woman should be expected to undertake the duties of surgeon and physician, chloroformist, dispenser, and nurse combined. Besides this, her own labour and influence are multiplied enormously when her assistant, a nurse, is a sister thoroughly in sympathy with her in her desire to win the souls of their patients to Christ.

Public sentiment in favour of women becoming medical students is being created and is an established thing in many of the cities of British India, and there are many girl students already in Medical Colleges. Lady Dufferin's Association's first aim is medical tuition, and her scheme is to train large numbers of women practitioners. But its avowed principle is philanthropic and not religious; and missionary training is cut off in all its institutions since it binds all associates not to speak to others on the subject of religion. Moreover, the atmosphere and surroundings of the students' boarding houses, mostly occupied by girls from homes where a low code of morals obtains, are undesirable. All honour to those Indian families of good position who, although non-Christian, hesitate to allow their daughters to study medicine in company with native men students, or to attend lectures given by native men.

With the desire of educated Christiau girls in Mission Boarding schools to adopt the medical or nursing profession, and to qualify themselves for Medical Mission work, the great need arose of a Christian Women's Medical College. For the companionship of Heathen and Mahommedan men and women students, together with the entire absence of all Christian teaching and influence, resulted so frequently in moral and spiritual failure that few of those who entered the Government course of study were, after its completion, fit or willing to take up Mission work. And the heads of the large Christian girls' schools had come to the decision that they could not in future allow their students to accept scholarships at the Government Medical schools.

In 1893, the idea of founding a Missionary School of Medicine in North India occurred to Miss Edith Brown, M.D., who has since been appointed as its first Principal. A permanent Committee was formed as an outcome of a conference of fourteen Medical Missionaries, representatives of seven Missionary Societies. In 1894, the C.E.Z.M.S., in committee assembled, passed a resolution in which they cordially approved of the establishment of such an undenominational College for the training of women and girls, and although unable to give any grant towards it, were prepared to arrange for the payment of any students' fees whom they might from time to time send to the college for training.

Ludhiana, as being the oldest scene of interdenominational Zenana work, was chosen as a site for the school. There is a large Hospital and Dispensaries, two of which are outlying, and the school itself is a large building in the Mission compound. Special contributions came in, and the institution was launched amid the gifts of many friends, among whom the Missionaries themselves rank first—always the first to give! Medical books and chemical apparatus came from the London School of Medicine for Women together with the promise of the gruesome, but indispensable, gift of a skeleton. The school started with seven girls, all learning nursing, and bid fair to prosper.

Since then the progress of the School has been very rapid. The students are, not only thoroughly trained medically by a competent staff of fully-qualified lady physicians, but they have regular Bible study and are prayerfully encouraged to become earnest and whole-hearted Missionaries, who will seek the salvation of their patients. The first Rule of Admission runs thus:—" Candidates must be decided Christians, and those holding Scholarships must undertake to work in

A Ludhiana Staff Nurse and her Little Patients.

some Protestant Mission to the Heathen after the completion of their course of study."

As many as forty girls are received at a time, and are being trained under five lady doctors and two English hospital-trained nurses, to become doctors, compounders, and nurses. The course for Hospital assistants covers four years, and that for compounders and nurses lasts two years. It argues well for the future to see these girls of different nationalities (for the students come from all parts of India) working so harmoniously over anatomy, physiology, chemistry, &c.,

and in the Hospital over dressings and other in-patient work. The course of instruction is given both in English and Urdu, but all the more educated girls know English very well.

No fewer than fourteen students with various qualifications, and some having obtained Government diplomas, passed out of the School and were located in different Mission Stations during 1900, one being appointed to an important post as helper in connection with the C.E.Z.M.S. at Sukkur.

There is every reason to hope that the students may soon have permission to enter the higher examinations in the Lahore University, the affiliation of the School being dependent on the accommodation for laboratories and the strength of its fully-qualified staff.

Testimonies that are constantly coming to hand prove that this important movement is being crowned with success. Two of the nurses sent recently to a Mission Hospital are found able to do all the evangelistic work, holding classes and having prayers for the servants, and in the Hospital (which they keep in beautiful order) one of them taking the Bible reading for the doctor, who is not as yet so fluent in Urdu.*

At present no such institution is established in China. Bnt although the difficulties are great and missionary effort in every direction is newer than in India, while necessarily British influence is wanting to strengthen philanthropic effort, the training of native women on medical lines by Missionary agencies is an established thing. Public opinion even in China has been created in favour of the medical profession for talented and enlightened women and self-supporting Chinese are taking up this department of work.

*Full particulars of the North India School of Medicine will be supplied by the Secretary, Miss M. W. Brown, 120 St. James' Road, West Croydon, Surrey.

Several Chinese lady doctors have completed a course of training and are practising professionally.

Eleven years ago a Chinese lady doctor appeared at Amoy, started a women's hospital, and showed the blessings that such a worker could diffuse. After passing through a medical course in the United States and winning honours over many of her fellow students, she came to Amoy in the care of her adopted father, a venerable American missionary.

It can never fail to excite interest that Chinese women are able, through education, to use their minds for the details of a study so long and so difficult to acquire as that of medicine and nursing.

Miss Mary Stone, M.D., a native of China, whose story is extremely interesting, has uttered the following weighty words which we cannot do better than quote *verbatim* :—" What scientific knowledge of medicine a few Chinese have acquired has been through the agency of Medical Missionaries, who, in addition to their practice, ranging annually from thousands to tens of thousands of patients, can scarcely be expected to find time or strength for much in the line of teaching. . . . . Nothing is convenient for a course of laboratory training in China. In a country where ancestors are worshipped, one does not wonder that dissection is interdicted. . . . In a country where women are not honoured, they are left to suffer untold miseries. In China there are women who would rather disease should run its course than call a man to treat them.

" As we cannot hope for enough foreign lady Missionaries to supply the needs of our women, or to train a sufficient number of Chinese women to be thoroughly qualified physicians, the only solution seems to be to send a number of Chinese women abroad to be educated, making them competent for independent work anywhere in China, even where foreigners cannot go. . . . To provide the means for any number of

Chinese girls to take such a course of study abroad, unless it be regarded as a legitimate field for Missionary effort, would require so much that I fear China will need to wait some generations yet for qualified medical women. . . . But do they (those trained in foreign countries) retain their connection with their own people, so that they are received in more intimate and more effective touch with the lives of the Chinese? A few items of personal experience may be pardoned here. Our reception by our people has been a source of surprise and gratification in more than one respect. . . . There has generally been a willingness to accept us and our work for what we could make manifest as true work. We are constantly brought in contact with great numbers of our countrywomen in a professional way, and all classes love to visit us at our Home, where we receive them and try in some way to speak a word or suggest an idea that will tell for Christian truth."

After the foregoing statements in our little book which have depicted in measure the woes of Chinese womanhood, we need not here emphasize the fact of the comfort which one of their own sisters as a doctor or nurse can impart. Anyone who understands Oriental life will take account of all this means, and fervently invoke blessing on those whom God is manifestly raising up to minister to their countrywomen.

Space does not allow of our dwelling longer on this extremely interesting and most important work—which in larger or smaller measure is being carried on in every one of the forty-four Hospitals and Dispensaries of our Society with equally blessed results. But may this slight sketch stir up much more definite prayer for trainers and trained, that our Eurasian, Indian, and Chinese sisters may be called and qualified by the Great Physician Himself in ever-increasing numbers to minister to multitudes between life and death.

* * * *

Our sketch of Women's Medical Mission work amongst women is finished. It is at best an imperfect outline of some only of the ministry that is being carried on by a noble army of healers that have gone forth into the battle which disease is waging in earth's darkest places.

Yet, compared with the vast area occupied by the foe, how few are the warriors! If 10,000 lady doctors went to India to-morrow, and another regiment of equal size were despatched to China, there is work —abundant, pressing work—for all in those two countries only.

But let us ever remember that the real remedy for which millions of our suffering sisters are waiting to-day is, not Western science, or a specific from the laboratory, or the miraculous skill of the operating room.

Their "open sore" in its deepest sense can never be healed by phial or lancet, or even tenderest human sympathy. It waits for the touch of Christ. The wounds and bruises of their sin-stained hearts can be mollified only by the balm of the Gospel. That name, which is "as ointment poured forth," must be heard and known and loved and trusted if their cry of pain is to cease. A redeeming God Himself must impart "health and cure." *Jehovah-rophi* is the unknown God, for a revelation of Whom the pain-worn, sin-sick women of the East wait.

And He waits to reveal Himself to them through those who give their feet to go, their eyes to see, their hearts to love, their hands to do, their time, their zeal, yea, themselves, to this Christ-like ministry of "pouring in oil and wine."

Christian woman, physician, surgeon, nurse, He waits for *you*.

Christian medical student, He waits for *you*.

Christian professional sisters the world over, He waits for *you*.

"The paths of pain are thine. Go forth
With patience, trust, and hope,
The sufferings of a sin-sick earth
Shall give thee ample scope.
That Good Physician liveth yet
Thy Friend and Guide to be;
The Healer by Gennesaret
Shall walk thy rounds with thee."

"God is no longer manifested in human form, going in and out among our sick ones. The hand of Christ is no longer laid on the fevered brow. It is for your hand to do that now and reduce the fever by all the means within your power. His touch of the sightless eyeballs does not to-day restore vision. He has commissioned you to do that with your cataract needle. The summer evenings, when the sick could be gathered at the door for the Master to heal, have sped away from the world's Capernaums; He is seeking to-day for representatives who shall go in Christ's stead and do His healing work, beseeching men to be reconciled to Him."

May no life of comfort and distinction loom so large that the Vision of Christ's beckoning hand shall not be seen. May His love—the only motive power strong enough to thrust forth to a life-service for His sake—constrain you to run on this sublimest and divinest errand.

For to you the promise holds good, "They shall lay hands on the sick and they shall recover." . . .

"SO THEY WENT EVERYWHERE, THE LORD WORKING WITH THEM, AND CONFIRMING THE WORD WITH SIGNS FOLLOWING."

W.S. Caine

'The Temperance Problem in India'. In C Yajnesvara Chintamani (ed), *Indian Social Reform*. Madras: Thompson and Co., 1901. 87-97

III.—The Temperance Problem in India.

By W. S. Caine, Esq., M. P.

The Temperance problem in India is almost entirely a product of British rule. The ancient Hindu no doubt had his own Temperance problem to solve. In the Vedas we find ample evidence of the drinking habits of the primitive Indo-Aryan who drank freely of the intoxicating juice of the sacred Soma or moonplant, with which he offered libations to his gods. But the Hindu was soon roused to a sense of the evil which he most manfully put down directly he became conscious of it. In the post-Vedic period of ancient Indian history, the strongest interdiction was put upon the use of all intoxicating liquors; and at a still later period when the great law books were compiled, the drinking of spirituous liquors was named as one of the five mortal sins which a Hindu could commit. The practice thus strongly forbidden came henceforth to be confined to the lowest and aboriginal classes of the Indian populations who were then practically outside the pale of the Hindu community. Later on, however, a new religious cult arose, called the Tantra, under which drink was associated with religious exercises. In the sixteenth century there arose in Bengal a great Brahmin prophet, Chaitanya, who absolutely prohibited the use of intoxicating liquors among his followers, giving them instead what he called "the new wine of Divine love," with which (we are told) he was himself constantly drunk and in which "he finally drowned himself." Like Buddha, Chaitanya raised a vigorous protest against caste and the ceremonial sacrifices which involved the use of strong liquors, and as a result of his preaching the Temperance problem, as it affected the lower classes of the population in Bengal, was effectively solved. This movement was still in progress when the

British went to India. But it cannot be said that it was helped by the British occupation. It is true that for the first twenty-five or thirty years after the East India Company was invested with sovereign power no excise regulations were set up. But the Government soon became aware that a considerable revenue might be derived from this source and accordingly in 1790-91 the first excise regulations were promulgated, ostensibly for the purpose of suppressing the evils of drunkenness and illicit distillation. The greater evil of Government sanction and control soon became evident.

In 1799, Mr. Wordsworth, the Magistrate and Collector of Rungpore, in Bengal, sent a representation to the Government complaining of the increase in drunkenness, and the numerous vicious practices that are universally associated with it, which he most distinctly attributed to the new Excise Regulations. Opinions of other magistrates were called for, who also, to a large extent, supported the views expressed by Mr. Wordsworth.

Practically nothing was done to change the policy of the Government, and the Excise system was gradually extended in one form and another until it covered the whole of the British dominions in India. The results were most deplorable. Liquor shops were opened all over the country. Officials of the Government openly encouraged the sale of drink, and the supreme authorities, blinded by considerations of revenue, did nothing to check the evil. Many Indian social reformers became alarmed at the prospect and urged the Government to introduce restrictions. They were so far listened to that a commission was appointed in 1883-84 to enquire into the liquor traffic in Bengal. Very little came of this commission although it had to admit, in its report, that not more than two-fifths of the growth of the revenues could be attributed to such normal causes as the growth of population and the increasing prosperity of the people. This report made it very clear that at least 50 per cent. of the increase in the Excise revenue was due to the action of the Government and its officials in forcing up revenues at the expense of the physical, social and moral welfare of the people.

I think I may claim to be the first Englishman who seriously investigated the Excise policy of the Indian Government. I made my first visit to India in the winter of 1887-88. My attention was drawn to the subject by a deputation which waited upon me in Bombay, consisting of some of the leading gentlemen of that city. They expressed a strong desire that some organization should be formed in England with a view to Parliamentary action, and also for the purpose of promoting and guiding an agitation throughout India for Temperance reform. I made some further enquiries into the matter, and convinced myself that India was threatened with all the *evil results* of the drink traffic with which we in this country are so familiar. On my return to England a meeting of members of Parliament and Temperance reformers was convened at the London residence of Mr. Samuel Smith, M.P., at which the Anglo-Indian Temperance Association was formed with the avowed object of resisting the spread of drinking facilities in India and of promoting total abstinence among the natives. Mr. Smith was elected President and I undertook the Secretaryship.

I returned to India in the following winter and made a prolonged tour with the Rev. Thomas Evans. We formed Temperance societies in nearly every place we visited and much enthusiasm was aroused in favour of Temperance reform. During this tour I made a complete study of the Excise administration of the country. I found that the methods of administration differed considerably in the various provinces, but that it was everywhere based upon what is known as the "farming system." This system still prevails in certain districts.

Licences for working distilleries of ardent spirits and opening liquor shops for their sale are granted for certain defined areas to the highest bidder. In some provinces the spirits are manufactured by the Government, and the right to retail only is let to farmers. The Government of India contended that this system was calculated to produce the maximum of revenue with a minimum of drunkenness; that the principles on which it was based were these—*viz.*: that liquor should be taxed and consumption restricted as far as it was possible to do so without imposing positive hardships upon the people and driving them to illicit manufacture. They contended that they had been completely successful in carrying out this policy, and that the great increase of Excise revenue, taken as evidence of drinking habits by those who only looked upon the surface, really represented a much smaller consumption of liquor and an infinitely better regulated consumption than prevailed in former years. I found this opinion maintained, with few exceptions, by the English official class in India; but in my intercourse with educated natives I found a strongly contrary opinion universal, and this was also held by every missionary with whom I came in contact. Native opinion maintains with great pertinacity that the increase of Excise revenue—which is still going on, as I shall presently show—represents a proportionate increase of intemperance throughout India; that the Government, under the thin pretence of suppressing illicit manufacture, are stimulating the extension of spirit licenses for revenue purposes; and that they have established liquor shops in a large number of places where formerly such things were unknown, in defiance of native opinion, to the misery and ruin of the population.

On my return to England steps were immediately taken to bring the matter under the notice of Parliament, and on 30th April 1889, Mr. Samuel Smith, M. P. moved the following resolution in the House of Commons :—

"That, in the opinion of this House, the fiscal system of the Government of India leads to the establishment of spirit distilleries, liquor and opium shops in large numbers of places, where, till recently, they never existed, in defiance of native opinion and protests of the inhabitants, and that such increased facilities for drinking produces a steadily increasing consumption, and spread misery and ruin among the industrial classes of India, calling for immediate action on the part of the Government of India with a view to their abatement."

I recorded the motion in a speech based upon the fact to which I have already referred and a long and interesting debate followed. Sir John Gorst, then Under-Secretary for India, speaking on behalf of the Government, met the resolution by a direct negative. The motion was also opposed by Sir Richard Temple, an ex-Governor of Bombay, and Sir James Fergusson, Under-Secretary for Foreign Affairs, who described it as "a very severe vote of censure on the Government of India." But in spite of this strong official opposition, and notwithstanding the fact that the Government had a large majority in the House, the resolution of censure was carried by 113 votes against 100, a majority of 13.

This was a great triumph for the cause of Temperance reform. The Secretary of State, Viscount Cross, sent a despatch to the Government of India embodying the resolution of the House of Commons. The Government of India took the matter up seriously, a thorough inquiry and investigation into the administration of the excise departments of the various provinces was instituted, and the defence of the Government of India was, after a lapse of eight months, published in a ponderous volume of 400 pages. That the policy of the Government was largely influenced by the resolution of the House of Commons will be seen by the following extract from the *Gazette of India*, 1st March 1890 :

"POLICY OF THE GOVERNMENT OF INDIA IN MATTERS OF EXCISE.

"103. Looking to all the conditions of the very difficult problem with which we have to deal, we have after careful consideration, arrived at the conclusion that the only general principles which it is expedient or even safe to adopt are the following :—

"(1) That the taxation of spirituous and intoxicating liquors and drugs shall be high, and in some cases as high as it is possible to enforce .

"(2) That the traffic in liquor and drugs should be conducted under suitable regulations for police purposes .

"(3) That the number of places at which liquor or drugs can be purchased should be strictly limited with regard to the circumstances of each locality ; and

"(4) That efforts should be made to ascertain the existence of local public sentiment, and that a reasonable amount of deference should be paid to such opinion when ascertained."

Thus the Government of India, always slow to move, at last instituted really serious reforms in many districts of the Indian Empire, and the alarming increase in the excise revenue was checked. But I regret to say that in recent years the excise revenue has again advanced. The effect of Parliamentary censure, I am afraid, has worn off and it is to be feared that the "general principles" set forth in the despatch already quoted, by which the excise department is professedly governed, are more often ignored than regarded. A comparison of the figures during the last twenty-five years will show how rapid the increase of the revenue has been :—

Net Excise Revenue of India

1874—75	1883—84	1894—95	1898—99
£1,755,000.	£2,840,000.	£3,965,000,	£4,127,000.

These figures reveal the startling fact that the revenue from intoxicants sold by a Christian Government to people whose religious and social habits are opposed to the sale of liquor and drugs altogether has more than doubled itself during the last twenty-five years, The figures themselves may seem small as compared with the consumption per head in Britain; but it must be borne in mind that the average income per head of the population in India is only one thirtieth that of the United Kingdom and that India is still practically a nation of total abstainers, the consumption being confined (at present, at any rate) to about fifty millions of the population.

As I have said, it is to be feared that the restrictive regulations of the Government of India have been considerably relaxed of late. Many instances of this have been brought to the notice of the Committee of the Anglo-Indian Temperance Association. Any sign of a diminishing revenue from excise appears to fill the officials of the department with grave alarm. One example of this is to be found in the last report on Excise in the Madras Presidency where it is stated that there has been a decrease in the consumption of liquor during the year 1898–99. And also a falling-off in the number of shops. Any satisfaction which the friends of Temperance in India might feel with regard to this is, however, neutralized by the comments which the Madras Government make in their review of this particular report, for we are told that "*it is to be doubted whether the reduction has not in some cases gone too far*"; and further that "the Board of Revenue has settled, in communication with collectors, the maximum and the minimum number of shops to be opened in each district." As this indicates a change of policy on the part of the Madras Government, and having regard to the fact that similar views are finding favour with some of the other provincial Governments, the reader will agree with me that the time has come when the attention of Parliament and the public ought once more to be directed to this matter. Mr. Samuel Smith, M. P., has accordingly placed the following notice of motion upon the order book of the House of Commons :—

"To call attention to the administration of Excise in India, by which many liquor-shops are being opened in various parts of India in direct violation of the expressed protests of the neighbourhood and in contradiction of the declared policy of the Government of India as formulated in their despatch to the Secretary of State, No. 29, February 4th, 1890, and to move a resolution."

In the meantime, however, the Total Abstinence work, carried on by the Anglo-Indian Temperance Association among the people of India, has made splendid progress. I have paid two more visits to India during the last ten years and more recently the General Secretary of the Anglo-Indian Temperance Association, Mr. F. Grubb, undertook a similar tour. As a result of these efforts a large number of Temperance societes have been established all over India. In this work we have been ably supported by the Rev. Thomas Evans, and by several influential vernacular lecturers, notably the Mahant Kesho Ram Roy, of Benares. This devoted Hindu was the means of inducing whole communities to prohibit the sale and consumption of strong drink among their members by caste rules. His death, which took place five years ago, was a great loss to the movement. In later years the Temperance cause has been admirably served by eloquent Indian lecturers, chief among whom have been Mr. Bipin Chandra Pal (Bengal) who was a delegate to the recent World's Temperance Congress, in London ; Mr. Shyam Kishore Varma (N. W. P., Oudh and Behar) ; and Mr. Yashwant Javagi Dabir (Bombay). As a result of these labours there are now in India 283 societies affiliated to the Association. There is hardly a town of any importance where some organization for the furtherance of Temperance principles does not exist. The societies are encouraged to hold regular meetings, to translate suitable Temperance tracts and articles from our quarterly journal "Abkari" into the vernaculars, to visit the surrounding villages, to submit memorials to Government against the opening of liquor shops, and generally to foster the growth of a sound Temperance sentiment among the people.

The progress of the movement would undoubtedly have been much more marked had it not been for the recurrent famines which have devastated India. These dire calamities have naturally diverted the attention of those influential workers to whom we have to look for the effective prosecution of the Temperance cause; for it must be remembered that the men who are taking the lead in this great movement are also in the forefront of every effort that is being made for the social and moral amelioration of the people of India. But although the struggle against famine and plague has made great demands upon the time and labours of some of our best helpers, the more permanent conflict between sobriety and intemperance has not been neglected by them. On the contrary, they realise that it is from the impoverished peasants of India that the greater portion of the Indian Excise Revenue is drawn, and that this is the very class which first succumbs to the privations imposed upon them in these recurring periods of scarcity.

The Excise reports for the past year have not yet been issued and it is therefore not possible to arrive at any conclusion as to the effect which the latest famine will have upon the Excise returns. At the end of the previous famine, however, I made a careful study of these returns and I found that for the first time for many years there was a marked decline in the next Excise receipts for the two years which were affected by the famine. Taking the Central Provinces as an example, in 1894-95 the net receipts from Excise were Rs. 27,21,007 while in 1896-97 they fell to Rs. 20,55,696, a drop of nearly 7 lakhs, or about 25 per cent. The Excise Commissioner, in his report, frankly attributed this falling off to famine; he wrote:—"In a famine year it is only natural that there should be a much smaller consumption by the public of Excise articles, and so the Revenue must fall." This was amply confirmed by reports from the districts. The Collector reported that the continued agricultural distress which made the liquor an unattainable luxury for the great bulk of the drinking class was the cause of the fall in receipts.

All this points to the melancholy conclusion that the customers of the liquor and drug shops of the Indian Government are mainly drawn from the very poorest strata of Indian society, 'that which falls at once into public relief at the first touch of famine. There can be no doubt that when the returns for the current year are issued this sad fact will be still further emphasised.

I invite the earnest attention of social reformers in India to the facts set forth above, and I appeal to them to lend their valuable aid to a movement which seeks to prevent their native land from falling under the baneful influence of a traffic which has wrought untold misery among the nations of the West, and which will, if not speedily checked, prove a no less potent instrument in the moral and social deterioration of the people of India.

John W.D. Megaw

'The Public Health Activities of the Government of India'. In Edward Blunt (ed), *Social Service in India: An Introduction to Some Social and Economic Problems of the Indian People*. London: His Majesty's Stationer's Office, 1938. 191-194.

The Public Health Activities of the Government of India

17. *Administration.*—By the Government of India Act of 1919 responsibility for medical relief and public health was transferred to the provincial Governments. Only a few subjects were retained under the control of the Government of India, such as legislation with regard to infectious diseases, external public health relations, port quarantine, statistics, and the medical research department. Under the present constitution, as laid down under the Government of India Act of 1935, the position remains much the same. The Government of India has now taken an important step which will bring it again into touch with public health activities in the provinces and so rectify a serious defect in the constitutional position. This step consists in the setting up in 1937 of a central Advisory Board of Health for the purpose of promoting coordination

* He found, for example, that a child who had been drowned was returned as having died of fever.

of effort between the provinces and States. This Board has no executive powers and therefore cannot encroach on the powers or responsibilities of the provincial Governments, but it is certain to have a great influence by providing for advice, consultation, and cooperation with regard to public health questions.

18. The Government of India has a small medical and public health section which is under the Member in charge of the department of Education, Health and Lands. The Director-General of the Indian Medical Service is the chief adviser to Government on all questions of a medical nature, while the Public Health Commissioner is his staff officer for public health. In technical matters the Public Health Commissioner is in direct relation with the other departments of the Government of India and with the provincial Governments when they seek his advice. He deals with vital statistics and produces an annual report, which is of great interest and importance ; he represents the Government of India on international health bodies, supervises the health of the major ports, and their quarantine work ; he deals with pilgrims, and is a member of many committees such as those of the Indian Red Cross Society, the British Empire Leprosy Relief Association and the King George's Anti-tuberculosis Fund. As secretary of the governing body of the Indian Research Fund Association and its Scientific Advisory Board, he is closely concerned with medical research. Not the least important of his duties are those connected with the new central Advisory Board of Health, of which he is secretary.

19. *Research.*—Although there was no regular organization of medical research till the early years of the present century, many great discoveries have been made by workers in India. The epoch-making discovery that malaria is conveyed from man to man by certain kinds of mosquitos is the best known of these. It was made by Surgeon-Major Ronald Ross, I.M.S.,* in 1898 as a result of pertinacious work carried out under great difficulties. Mention may also be made of the discovery by Leonard Rogers † of emetine as a cure for amoebic infection and of the modern treatment of cholera, and of the great additions made to our knowledge of malaria by Richard

* The late Sir Ronald Ross, K.C.B., K.C.M.G.

† Major-General Sir Leonard Rogers, K.C.S.I., C.I.E., F.R.S. (I.M.S. retired).

Christophers.* These men have achieved international fame for their work; but there are many others, both Indians and Europeans, who have rendered great services to India and the rest of the world by their discoveries in connexion with plague, *kala azar*, leprosy, cholera, malaria, and a host of other diseases. There are thousands of people in India who owe their lives to the patient researches which have been carried out by this band of workers.

20. The Government of India, although its public health department has only a small staff of three technical experts, at the present time is following a progressive and enlightened policy in connection with medical research. It maintains a medical research department with a staff of twenty-six workers, who are recruited partly from the Indian Medical Service and partly from outside sources. The work is done in the central research institute at Kasauli, the all-India institute of hygiene at Calcutta, and in a number of provincial institutes to which members of the department are deputed. India has six Pasteur institutes—at Kasauli, Coonoor, Bombay, Patna, Calcutta, and Shillong.† These, in addition to treating persons bitten by rabid dogs, have recently begun to distribute anti-rabic vaccine to local centres so that preventive treatment against rabies is rapidly becoming available to patients within easy reach of their homes. These institutes are maintained by the provincial Governments with the exception of that at Kasauli, which is managed by a committee. Nearly 45,000 patients were treated in India and Burma in 1934.

21. The Research Fund Association, founded in 1911, is financed by the Government of India, and is administered by a governing body with official and non-official members. The governing body is advised by a Scientific Advisory Board composed of medical experts. The amount spent by the Association on research has varied between seven and twelve lakhs of rupees yearly.‡ Numerous important investigations have been carried out in connection with the great killing diseases of India. The Association maintains two very important organizations, the malaria survey of India and the nutritional research laboratories. The malaria survey, which will

* Brevet-Colonel Sir Richard Christophers, Kt., C.I.E., O.B.E. (I.M.S. retired).

† There is a seventh at Rangoon in Burma.

‡ Between £52,500 and £90,000.

in future be called the malaria institute, has a budget of some two lakhs of rupees (£15,000). It carries out research work on malaria, advises the Government of India and provincial Governments in connection with anti-malarial measures, and trains medical men in practical malaria work; it also publishes a large number of important papers every year. The work of the experts in this department is recognized as being of great value to India and the whole world. The Government of India has recently distributed a large amount of quinine (45,000 lb.) to provincial Governments to supplement the amount which they had previously been distributing for the treatment of malaria; and during the year 1936 it also gave to the Association a special grant of 10 lakhs (£75,000) for anti-malaria work, which will be used on the maintenance of anti-malaria projects in certain areas. Nutritional research is recognized to be of very special importance to India, and about a lakh of rupees (£7,500) yearly has been spent on it in recent times.

22. The all-India institute of hygiene is maintained by the Government of India for research and training in public health. The Calcutta school of tropical medicine and the hospital for tropical diseases owe their existence to the enlightened and persistent efforts of Sir Leonard Rogers. The school receives an indirect subsidy from the Government of India, but is maintained by the Government of Bengal and by an endowment fund provided by the Jute, Tea, and Coal-mining Associations as well as by private benefactors. This school originally included an institute of hygiene, but thanks to the generosity of the Rockefeller Foundation the all-India institute of hygiene was provided with separate accommodation in a fine building. It still works in close collaboration with the school of tropical medicine, but is now financed by the Government of India. The two institutions, in addition to carrying out important research work, prepare students for the diploma and licence given by the State Faculty of Tropical Medicine of Bengal, for the D.P.H. of the Calcutta University, and for other examinations.

C.F. Strickland

'Voluntary Effort and Social Welfare.' In Edward Blunt (ed), *Social Service in India: An Introduction to Some Social and Economic Problems of the Indian People*. London: His Majesty's Stationer's Office, 1938. 380-398.

Voluntary Associations in India

14. The structure of Indian society was eminently well suited to serve the welfare of all classes, except the depressed castes,* in the circumstances which surrounded the Indian individual before contact with Europe. The caste, whether in the looser form of a number of persons who might be widely scattered but were related or believed to be related to one another by blood, or in the closer form of a professional guild, assured to each man the assistance of caste fellows † through his life and at his death and met the needs of which he was conscious. Apart from certain religious observances,‡ he was not conscious of a need for detailed regulation of the public health, though some sort of drainage in the cities was frequently provided, by the householder for his house and by authority for the streets, from the days of Mohenjo-Daro onwards. Nor, again, was the ordinary man conscious of a need for education as now understood. He enjoyed a cultural knowledge of scripture and poetry; but his profession was predetermined, and literature and learning were the privileges of certain castes whose members lived by their possession and use. Agricultural improvement consisted in the fencing of crops against wild animals, the sinking of wells, and the breaking up of waste land. Primitive associations for such objects were no doubt created and dissolved as occasion arose, but farmers who cultivated principally for their own subsistence were little inclined to scientific research or to the production of a surplus for which there was no market. Broadly speaking, therefore, the Indian individual up to 200 years ago—and indeed much later—was not required to join with his neighbours in voluntary associations. The village meeting and his caste were non-

* See Chapter II, paras. 19, 46–47.

† This assistance would, in practice, be rendered by the *biradari*; see Chapter II, para. 18.

‡ See Chapter II, para. 43.

voluntary associations, into which he was born and which controlled whatever the ordinary man could hope to control. Beyond them lay an inscrutable earthly ruler and the inscrutable forces of nature and of God.

15. In this general account one exception must be allowed. The early savings associations—*Nidhis*, *Chit* funds,* and various kinds of *anjuman* †—offered an opportunity of thrift to those who handled cash, i.e. for the most part the town-dwellers. They admitted only too often an element of chance which is incompatible with true thrift, but were not without value. The rural population dealt less often in cash, and the accumulation of grain or other food beyond the owner's requirements was, while communications were scanty and insecure, an idle occupation.

16. The idea, therefore, of lasting association with other individuals for the common good, as distinguished from temporary collaboration for a specific act of construction or production, only became familiar to India when commercial crops could be sold, when the proceeds could be spent on luxuries hitherto unknown or unattainable, when education opened a road to advancement in official or private occupations, and when medical science revealed the possibility of living more comfortably and living longer; in other words, when under British rule the country was pacified, a regular administration was established, trade began to expand, and scientific knowledge of the causes of health and sickness to be acquired. It was not unnatural, then, that voluntary associations should come but slowly into existence, and first in the urban areas, where European influence was most strongly felt. Social reform was in the early part of the nineteenth century ancillary to religious change, especially among Hindus, whose social and religious ideas are so intimately interconnected. The Brahmo Samaj and later the Arya Samaj,‡ two outstanding Hindu movements, showed marked signs of reaction to European influence, as well as of independent Hindu thought, in the religious, social, and political fields; but Muslim society remained comparatively little affected before the closing

* See Chapter X, para. 11, and note.

† Assembly or society.

‡ The Brahmo Samaj was a religious sect, founded by Ram Mohan Roy in 1828. Its doctrine was theistic, and on the social side its objects were the spread of English education, the reform of the Hindu family, and the abolition of *sati*. For the spread of English education, see Chapter VIII, para. 3. For the Arya Samaj, see Chapter II, para. 33.

decades of the century. From that time forward the principle of individual action through association for the common good—not only the good of the family, caste, or tribe—was increasingly applied by Indians, and was instilled into students at the universities and in the higher schools. The caste or tribal organizations, though vital and powerful in many personal matters, were inappropriate for business concerning India as a whole, and voluntary associations of the English type began to appear.

17. The most numerous and most highly integrated body of voluntary associations are the co-operative societies, to which a previous chapter has been devoted. It is, however, necessary to remind the reader of their prominent place in the sphere of social welfare. As already explained, many associations which in Europe lie outside the co-operative fold lie within it in India, precisely because an association for social welfare is still a novelty and there is advantage in securing for it a framework and a backing which will induce its members and other people to regard it as a recognized institution and treat it seriously. We shall not, however, discuss co-operative societies here as a separate class. A social end may be achieved without co-operative registration as well as with it, *provided that* the members of a group hold together, observe the rules which they have laid down for themselves, including the payment of promised subscriptions, and actually carry on the work which they have undertaken to carry on.* Nor shall we discuss the operations of the several " beneficent " or " nation-building " departments of Government, as they are frequently called in India ; for these too have been set out in the preceding chapters. We are here only concerned with voluntary societies for the purpose of social welfare, and the coordination of such societies amongst themselves and with the departments of Government. The simplest method is to select, in the first place, a few unofficial bodies from various parts of India and to describe their work.

18. The Bengal central co-operative anti-malarial † society of Calcutta, founded in 1912 by Dr. G. C. Chatterjee and reorganized in 1919 as a central institution of the anti-malarial societies which he and his friends were creating in the villages,

* It should be remembered that in India, as in most other countries, only a *registered* co-operative society may call itself co-operative. The law of England does not impose this useful restriction.

† For malaria, see Chapter VII, paras. 6 *et seq.*

has now some 2,000 such dependent bodies affiliated to it. About half of these are registered co-operative societies. The anti-malarial movement aims at bringing together parties of men and women who believe in self-help and discard the fatalist view that malaria is unavoidable and an act of God. Before medical research had traced its origin to the anopheles mosquito, this disease was held to be due to evening mists arising from water, especially from stagnant water ; and Bengal being peculiarly subject to floods from the rivers and water-courses, the people saw no remedy for their affliction. Dr. Chatterjee and his disciples proceeded to impress on the villagers that the teaching of officials and doctors concerning the mosquito was really true, and to form societies for filling up swampy depressions, oiling pools, and taking quinine. All this had been preached by health experts for years ; but it was not until an unofficial and unpaid propagandist came to him in his home that the illiterate, suspicious, and apathetic peasant could be moved to action. The floods of Bengal in themselves brought no malaria, provided the water did not remain in stagnant pools and swamps in which the mosquito could breed. Consequently, the later efforts of the anti-malarial societies have been directed towards freeing the watercourses from unauthorized and unregulated dams, above which the water stood stagnant. Engineering schemes of this nature are expensive, and the voluntary societies, through their central society, have rightly turned to the Bengal Government for technical advice and financial help. These have been forthcoming, and the control of floods by this collaboration between voluntary and unofficial agencies has benefited considerable areas and afforded a striking example of co-ordinated welfare work. The village anti-malarial societies have also in some cases been supported by the union boards in the maintenance of local dispensaries, but many boards are uninterested, and much yet remains to be done. The central society derives its income from annual subscriptions and from the endowments collected and invested by Dr. Chatterjee, but its resources are small in comparison with the task before it.

19. An urban institution of value in Calcutta is the Bengal Social Service League. This body, founded in 1915, conducts an industrial school, a school of popular education, and some adult schools to combat illiteracy. It promotes agricultural conferences, carries on co-operative propaganda, and organizes

relief on the occasion of floods and famines. The first Indian social conference of 1916 was due to the initiative of the league. Its income proceeds from subscriptions and from government grants, but popular support is not yet sufficient to allow the promoters to do much outside Calcutta itself. Nevertheless it is evidence of a growing spirit of social service in India. Similar bodies, such as the Seva Sadan, may be found in other Indian cities; all are of recent date, for the new spirit is that of the new generation.

20. Two other Bengal organizations deserve attention. Firstly, the women's institutes (*Mahila samitas*) affiliated to the Saroj Nalini Dutt Association and through it allied with the women's institutes of England and the world, number several hundreds in Bengal and Assam, with outlying societies in other provinces and Ceylon. They are found for the most part in rural towns, and encourage their members in the study and practice of handicrafts, horticulture, education, and hygiene. Organizers from the central association visit the local institutes; a monthly magazine is also published. The movement is notable not so much for what it has hitherto achieved, as for the natural and healthy outlet which Indian women enjoy in it for self-expression and for self-education in questions of domestic and social interest. Joint societies of men and women are not yet congenial to India, but in the atmosphere of an institute the Indian woman, urban or rural, feels free to speak and to learn. The women's co-operative societies in the Punjab and the United Provinces, some 300 in each case, are really women's institutes under another name.

21. The second Bengali organization is that of Bratachari, which in the last few years has begun to revive popular songs and dances and to bind its members in a national or community movement for knowledge, labour, truth, unity, and joy. The pledge includes promises to be kind to animals, to live by the labour of one's body, to smile in misfortune, and *not* to develop a corporation! Bratachari may be compared on the one side with the Boy Scouts and on the other with the folksong and dance societies of Europe.

22. Prominent among societies for children in all parts of India are the Boy Scouts, numbering about 250,000; the parallel army of *Seva Samiti*; and the Junior Red Cross with 400,000 members, in which children are trained in ideas of health and service. The competition or overlapping of these

three movements is regrettable. All are good, and the record of boys who have assisted at religious festivals,* where masses of people are crowded in a narrow space, has been very creditable. Girl Guides are less numerous, because of the limitations on the freedom of girls and of early marriage; but they are advancing, and training camps are now regularly arranged for them. Camps for boys are also regularly held.

23. Associations in a somewhat different category are those which concentrate their energies on a village "centre" and hope to produce within this narrow range so obvious an improvement that adjacent villages will spontaneously imitate them or at least ask for advice. As an example we may take Khed Shivapur in Poona district, where for a series of years the Deccan Agricultural Association, in alliance with the Poona Seva Sadan and the Servants of India society, has carried on propaganda for better agriculture, health, and female education. A gymnasium and a demonstration farm, a midwife and a sewing class, a Marathi magazine and a free library are all part of the picture. Appreciable results are obtained in "centres" of this kind if the propaganda is continued for many years and if a trained and intelligent organizer resides in the village. Otherwise the effect tends to be transient.

24. Rural reconstruction centres on the same lines are attached to the Bombay co-operative institute and the Madras co-operative union. A Supervisor, ordinarily paid though not on the scale of his possible earnings in another occupation, is posted in each village and builds up a local committee. There being few voluntary societies in Indian villages, the members of the committee serve in a personal capacity and seldom represent, as they would in an English village, a club or association having a special object. If the local response has been cordial and local leaders appear to be forthcoming, the Supervisor is sooner or later transferred to a new centre and the welfare work of his village is left in the hands of a young men's association. This is the ideal outcome of concentrated work in a "centre," since a welfare organizer cannot be placed by Government or voluntary societies in each of the 660,000 villages of India. It is essential that: (1) the local committee be backed by a sufficiently large progressive (but not too radical) element among the population, if it is not to be defeated by the stolidity of the last-ditch conservatives; and (2) contact

* E.g. the *Kumbh Melas*: see Chapter VII, para. 34.

be retained with a central organization at a district or provincial headquarters, by which guidance and information may from time to time be supplied.

25. We have referred to several types of local institutions, urban or rural, each of which occupies itself either with a single kind of welfare activity over a relatively large area or with all kinds of welfare work in a small area. Reconstruction on a national scale, however, postulates a combination of all kinds of welfare activity at the same time in the whole of India, though such action need not be directed from a single point. In view of the great size of India, the province or the Indian State is probably a better unit of management; and since voluntary and official efforts should for reasons of effectiveness and economy be coordinated, a provincial or State scheme, put into force through district branches and village committees, is more likely to extract the maximum result than either an intensively centralized national and all-India scheme or a multiplicity of small local institutions which proceed from no general idea and arrive at no common end. The mean has to be preserved between an excessive stimulation and control by authority, which would hamper the initiative of private citizens, and an undue detachment of voluntary societies from official help with which they ought to be linked.

26. The most striking example of voluntary welfare organization in India, in which the initiative, the driving force, and most of the cost are provided by non-official persons and bodies, is the rural demonstration centre of the Y.M.C.A. at Martandam in the south of Travancore State. Here and at a few similar centres in Madras presidency, such as Ramanathapuram in the Nilgiris and Indukurpet in Nellore, the Y.M.C.A. has established a rural station at which better agriculture and handicrafts, co-operative methods in credit, marketing, and production, juvenile and adult education, including recreation and the drama, scout and guide training, and health and sanitation, are taught in practice as well as in theory. The Martandam centre owes much to the leadership of Dr. Spencer Hatch, an American, and its influence now extends to more than one hundred surrounding villages, where Y.M.C. Associations have been set up for propaganda and welfare activities on the same plan as at Martandam; but inquiries and visitors arrive from much further afield. The institution in charge of the work in each case, however, is the

village rural development association, of which persons of every religion, caste, and community are members ; the Y.M.C.A. is an important force in the organization of public opinion, but is not essential to the plan. No religious distinctions are introduced into social welfare.

27. Four points emerge from the plan of the Martandam rural development association : points to which we shall recur when examining other plans, and which are prime elements of success in any scheme of rural reconstruction.

28. (1) The attack on the rural problem is made all along the line. It would be unjust to regard as valueless those partial treatments of rural poverty and backwardness, which are adopted by some agricultural experts, credit co-operators, doctors, schoolmasters, or others. They are not valueless, but half their potential value is lost through the narrowness of their front. A small farmer cannot or will not accept new seed, improved implements, or methods of cultivation, or buy, breed, and maintain better livestock so long as he is indebted, illiterate, and constantly sick through malaria or hook-worm. He will not collaborate loyally with his fellows and impose on himself the discomforts of co-operative credit, such as limitation of expenditure on ceremonies and publicity in respect of loans, so long as, in addition to being illiterate and sick, he is unable to extract from his land, through faulty agriculture, more than the barest subsistence. Nor will he open his mind to adult education or send his children to school regularly for at least six years if he is sick, indebted, and poor ; on a low scale of living the ignorant man fares as well as the wise. Medical and hygienic precautions, again, seem to him weird if not impious ideas, a defiance of the will of Heaven, so long as he is dulled by the burden of debt, half-starved, and ignorant. Consequently the remedy—not a simple remedy—for the social evils of India is to combine an increase of income and relief from old debt with an opening of his mind in youth and in mature age, and with a release from stomach-aches, head-aches, and lassitude. All the evils which beset the poor man in India, and in lesser degree also the more prosperous man, must be dealt with at the same time, his friends uniting in a concerted effort to show him that his life *as a whole*, even on the modest plane of an artisan, labourer, or peasant-farmer, might be something different from and better than that which it now is. Accounts of other countries may give him courage,

successful experiments in communal improvement in India will convince him that a change is possible. Then he will believe, and begin to move his own hands and feet for himself. And the same is true of his wife.

29. Now one great virtue of the Martandam plan is that it proceeds on a broad front, or, to change the metaphor, pierces the vicious circle in which thousands of Indian peasants and labourers revolve at a number of different points on the circumference. While ploughs and poultry add to the village's income, co-operative credit and marketing reduce his losses; literacy, followed by libraries and craft schools, fits him to seize new opportunities; bored-hole latrines, ventilators, windows, and quinine render him and his wife and children stronger to do their daily business.

30. (2) The agents and propagandists of rural development are trained for their task. This has been a comparatively rare feature of social welfare work in India in the past; devoted men have plunged into a sea of difficulties without preparation and have learned only by painful experience how to surmount them. It should be remembered that in such cases the pain of the experience is not confined to the welfare worker, but is shared by those whom he is trying to help. Unfortunately, a course of all-round training for such persons is not easily obtained in India, and though facilities for an urban course are not entirely lacking in Bombay, rural training cannot well be given in a city. Martandam and Ramanathapuram have now for some years conducted rural courses of five or six weeks, attracting students from other parts of India as well as from Travancore and Madras. They are practical rather than theoretical, and a considerably longer period of study is really required by those who are to carry responsibility in any social welfare scheme; but the principle of employing trained men and women for social welfare is recognized and applied in these Y.M.C.A. centres, and is of fundamental importance.

31. (3) In the third place, welfare work in order to be worth doing should be not only broadly conceived, not only carried on by a trained personnel who will avoid the blunders committed by untrained organizers all over the world, but should also aim at making its results permanent. Only too often enthusiastic individuals after attaining results which appeared splendid have lost their zeal or been removed from the scene, and it has then become plain that the whole achieve-

ment depended on their presence and collapses in their absence. Since, therefore, the Indian peasant or labourer cannot in a few years, probably cannot in a single generation transform his outlook and his habits, social welfare work, and particularly rural welfare work, must during the interval be promoted and sustained by an institution which is itself permanent. It must *not* depend on individuals who may very shortly disappear. The only permanent bodies which can fulfil this function are (i) Governments, and (ii) voluntary associations having a stable existence, an adequate income to pay their staff, and a continuous policy. In the past the majority of the latter have been Christian, but there is no reason why non-Christian societies, such as the "Servants of the Untouchables" or village industries associations, should not be equally successful. The two types of agency—Governments and voluntary societies—will effect most if they remain in touch with one another and work as allies. Government departments are permanent, but cannot always reach the people; voluntary societies reach the people, but may lack resources or knowledge which Governments can supply. The Y.M.C.A., moreover, in its "centres" relies on local committees of the people in order to create and foster a real demand for social changes which will be permanent because the people make them their own. Ultimately the local associations should be able to stand by themselves, calling in an officer of Government or an employee of the Y.M.C.A. (or other central institution) when required, but not depending throughout on such persons for initiative. This will take time, but the Y.M.C.A. is stable and has a continuous policy. It is in alliance with the officers of Travancore State and of British districts, and while its leaders would be the first to admit that they have not won their battle or done all that they hope to do, the Martandam plan stands out as an example of welfare work so steady and so well coordinated with official effort that it should be studied and imitated wherever possible in India.

32. (4) Lastly, the cost is low, and while high-grade experiments, such as the Rockefeller health units, may well be worth while on account of the special information derived from them, India cannot afford, nor is it intended, to multiply them throughout the country. Martandam and the other centres avoid expensive buildings and plant. Grants are annually made to Martandam by Travancore State and to Kosamba centre by Baroda State; another part of the cost is borne by

the Y.M.C.A.; there is income from handicrafts and some subscriptions; but the bulk of the work in the villages themselves is carried on by local honorary people, many of them modest in education and status. This is what India can afford; and provided that honorary welfare-workers are themselves trained to a certain point and are guided by persons, official or non-official, of higher training, the plan is capable of indefinite extension at a relatively small cost.

Official Schemes of Rural Development

33. From voluntary associations let us now turn to official schemes. Clearly a Government commands experts and resources on a scale with which those of other institutions cannot be compared, and if it is recognized that in social welfare the government servant suffers from certain handicaps —he may be over-influential, he has many other occupations, he may be transferred from the locality—and that unofficial help is indispensable in order to make individual citizens really act on expert advice and learn the nature of their difficulties, then under the conditions of India today a social welfare scheme, directed and financed by the provincial or State Government and carried into effect through semi-official district bodies and voluntary village committees, is more likely to succeed in producing useful results than either a number of keen but isolated departments or a medley of uncoordinated voluntary societies without money or trained staff.

34. Four provinces of India have now a provincial scheme of rural development or welfare. The Punjab set up in 1923 a rural community board in Lahore, under a minister as chairman, and with the heads of rural departments and of the major unofficial organizations, such as the Red Cross, as members. In each district was established a district community council (now called the Dehat Sudhar committee) with the District Officer as chairman and the local departmental officers and leading non-official persons as members. The object was to coordinate the activity of the departments and of voluntary welfare or economic institutions, where such existed. Finance was provided by a grant from the Punjab Government to the board and from local subscriptions to the councils. Joint propagandist meetings were arranged in the villages, lectures were given, travelling cinemas and lantern slides were procured, and a certain impetus was given to the improvement of agriculture, health, female education, drama, singing, and

recreation. The weaknesses here, as in other provinces, proved to be the preoccupation of the District Officer with other duties, the deficiency of voluntary associations in the rural areas, and the reluctance of the people to form them or otherwise to participate in the campaign except under official pressure. Many councils still function with greater or less vigour, but inter-departmental meetings of officers or "Officers' Boards" in each district have to some extent overshadowed them and left some of them without motive power.

35. A remarkable campaign of "uplift" was conducted for seven years in Gurgaon district near Delhi by the District Officer, Mr. F. L. Brayne, in which, while the district community council was not ignored, the greater part of the work done was due to the force and zeal of Mr. Brayne himself. The achievements of this seven-year experiment impressed public opinion throughout India and in other regions of the world, and it was demonstrated that even in a backward district the people could be led or driven by an officer whom they trusted and liked to accept changes in agricultural methods and social customs, and to abandon many unhygienic or uneconomic practices. They would also subscribe money for social objects of which they approved. The influence of Gurgaon on Indian social policy has been marked and lasting. On the other hand it soon became evident, on Mr. Brayne's departure from the district, that little permanent mark had been left on Gurgaon itself, and that slower progress with more attention to the development of unofficial committees and institutions, which might in the future function with less official stimulation, would in the end be more secure. This lesson has been learned and applied in varying degrees in the Bombay, Central Provinces, and United Provinces schemes. The Punjab Government subsequently posted Mr. Brayne as Commissioner of Rural Reconstruction to encourage government servants, community councils, and all other agencies in the work of rural welfare. The Commissioner, in his publications and otherwise, lays great stress on the need for (1) female education,* without which the progress of men and boys must be halting and slow; (2) the co-operative movement, in which those who desire to make progress may support and pledge one another; and (3) *panchayats* and other village institutions, which in every country are indispensable as the focus of progressive opinion and the organ of action. An

* Cf. Chapter II, paras. 57–58.

awakening has, for the time at least, taken place in the villages of the Punjab, but it is uncertain how far the Dehat Sudhar committees have rooted themselves in the life of the people, how far they are capable of spontaneous activity. There is no parallel organization in the towns ; its creation is much to be desired.

36. Bengal has appointed a Development Commissioner and passed a Development Act, but the line of advance is more strictly economic than in the Punjab. Shortly after the formation of the rural community board and the district councils in the Punjab, reconstruction in rural areas was begun in certain districts of the Central Provinces and the United Provinces. In the year 1930 Pipariya, in Hoshangabad district (Central Provinces), and a cirle of fifty adjacent villages—later reduced to thirty—were selected for an intensive welfare campaign, to which the officers of the agricultural, co-operative, education, health, and veterinary departments devoted special attention. Here, as in the other schemes to be described in other provinces, the improvement of agriculture (e.g. the use of better ploughs, seed, and implements, the sowing of cotton in lines instead of broadcast), the consolidation of holdings, the reorganization of co-operative societies, the promotion of adult schools, rural libraries, and scout troops, the digging of refuse pits or bored-hole latrines, vaccination, and better housing, were all recommended to the people and introduced if a response was met.* Additional staff was employed, joint meetings of officers and non-official leaders were held, and since the Pipariya scheme was an experiment, extra expense was incurred. After two years the plan was enlarged, and a village uplift board was constituted by the Central Provinces government at Nagpur, with district uplift committees in the districts. Non-official members were included, and in some districts private citizens were found to be excellent agents for propaganda on behalf of village welfare. A minor campaign was conducted in Drug district, where consolidation of holdings was a prominent feature. The debt conciliation boards,† a somewhat later development, have already been mentioned.

37. The first steps in the United Provinces were taken in the Benares, Fyzabad, Lucknow, and Partabgarh districts

* The detailed improvements recommended in a scheme will not be enumerated again. They are much the same, though with local differences of stress, in all rural development in India.

† See Chapter X, para. 27.

with the formation of "centres" and rural reconstruction societies by the co-operative department. All other departments then joined in the campaign, and the publicity officers took charge of the propaganda and the touring motor-vans with slides, cinemas, and broadcasting.* The United Provinces Government created a rural development board for the province and a rural development association for each district. At headquarters they placed a Rural Development Officer, who was in general charge of development operations. In the districts they created an establishment of inspectors and organizers under the general supervision of an officer of the district staff, also designated Rural Development Officer, who did this work in addition to his other duties. In each district six circles of twelve villages are now chosen for intensive propaganda, each with an organizer, who is, however, to be supervised by a local citizen or officer of higher status. Where possible, village associations are brought into being and *panchayats*, with a legal constitution under the *Panchayat* Act, are utilized for the general support of the movement. An interesting and peculiar element in the United Provinces scheme is that the numerous tube wells that had been built in the large tract covered by the hydro-electric grid † are used as centres for the provision of certain suitable amenities in the shape of bathing-pools, a supply of drinking-water which is kept in tanks and drawn off by hydrants, places for watering cattle, and occasionally swimming-pools. At a certain number of the wells loud-speakers have been installed which are served by the radio station at Delhi, and provide suitable programmes in which instruction and amusement are carefully blended. A feature of these programmes is the market prices.

38. *Taluka* development associations had existed for many years in Bombay presidency. Their duty was to encourage agricultural improvements, but their effectiveness and worth varied with the circumstances of each district and with changes in the local staff. In 1933 a village improvement scheme for the presidency was initiated by Sir Frederick Sykes, Governor of Bombay. No central board is contemplated in this scheme, and though the appointment of a Village Improvement Officer under each of the three divisional Commissioners was approved, it does not appear that such appointments have been made. The work of social welfare is primarily rural, and therefore

* See Chapter V, para. 7, *note*.
† See Chapter V, para. 42, *note*.

entrusted to district committees, of which the District Officer is chairman, with *taluka* committees and village associations. Coordination may be secured either through the divisional Commissioners or through the heads of the rural and other departments, who may address their own officers and through them the district committees. The reports indicate that many minor developments and improvements are proceeding, and since the Indian village is a small unit which receives great benefit from minor local works, there can be no doubt that the total benefit is considerable.

39. In the last three years the Government of India has set aside large sums (nearly £3,000,000) for grants to provincial Governments in aid of rural improvements. Water-supply and sanitation, provision of better cattle and live stock, rural roads and consolidation of holdings were particularly specified by the Government, but grants have also been sanctioned for other purposes of a similar nature, and a certain portion was allocated to co-operative training and education. This money will facilitate rural welfare work, but involves no alteration of policy. The provincial Governments of Bombay, the Central Provinces, and the United Provinces are applying their allotments to their provincial schemes already in force.

40. It would be a grave mistake to demand from any scheme, whether mainly under official or non-official leadership, an early crop of visible results. The outlook of an adult is not easily readjusted, and if he or she lives in a remote village and is illiterate, readjustment is even more painful and laborious. For this reason social reformers in India have rightly tried to teach and train the children. Much is being done in schools, Scout and Guide troops, and junior Red Cross societies; and Mr. Brayne's organization of children in Gurgaon was powerful. The Y.M.C.A. in south India, the several "centres" of voluntary bodies such as the Deccan agricultural association, and the main provincial schemes, while doing all that they can for the present, hope for greater return from their labours when the young generation grows up in an atmosphere of new ideas. We have therefore to envisage not a brief and brilliant campaign, but a sustained policy of welfare work for a generation or longer; and the provincial and other schemes have all to be examined in the light of this principle.

41. (1) Are they co-ordinating all available forces, official and unofficial, and advancing on a broad front? To this we may answer that all departments are collaborating, every rural evil is being attacked, and those unofficial institutions which are non-political are brought into the scheme. It is inconvenient for a government, of whatever complexion, to ally itself with a political body which is also active in the cause of social welfare, since a government in such cases is open to criticism by opponents of the political view in question; though if the welfare work of any group is entirely divorced from its political activity, a large-minded government should be able to join hands with it. There is less certainty as to the share which private citizens are able to take in the business and responsibilities of the district committees, since there the departmental officers, who have a clear departmental policy and may be reluctant to amend it, play a large part. In village associations the private individual is obviously on strong ground, if an organizer is not impatient and does not carry too much of the load himself, and on the provincial board, where such exists, representatives of voluntary societies and even of political groups ought to be able to help. The weak spot is the district committee. If not nursed into strength, it may sink to a position of unimportance, merely endorsing the decisions of officers or officers' boards. Voluntary societies will then be unable to come into being or to function.

42. (2) Are the provincial schemes likely to produce permanent results? Will a time come, after one or even two generations, when social welfare work will depend in greater degree on the will and in less degree on the assent, cordial or resigned, of the people? The same question as to the co-ordination of official and unofficial work and the evocation of an increasing response from the people, which we were considering in the preceding paragraph, arises here also. Economic depression or political change may at any moment cause a contraction of expenditure by the Governments concerned or a diversion of official staff in other directions. Results will be permanent if and in so far as, when this occurs, private citizens and voluntary societies are ready to fill the gap. Some such voluntary bodies are at work—we have referred to a few of them—and in the provincial, district, and village boards and committees unofficial aid is enlisted. The permanence of the impression made on the social life of India will correspond with the reality of the part assigned to such persons and

associations. Even at the price of moving more slowly—and if the voluntary, sometimes less fully instructed, social workers are to keep pace, the pace must be slower than that of trained and zealous officers—it is essential to use voluntary agency more and more. This policy is accepted by all the Governments and is no doubt being adopted in practice by the more long-sighted authorities and individuals.

43. (3) Some training is being given to social workers in the three rural schemes of Bombay, the Central Provinces, and the United Provinces. Local classes for short periods have been held, but it is difficult to believe that the majority of organizers, guides, and inspectors have yet received the training which they require. It is not sufficient to call together the organizers for two or three weeks and explain to them the arguments in favour of better ploughs, bored-hole latrines, a later age of marriage, or co-operative thrift ; this has been done everywhere, and perhaps most fully in the United Provinces. There is still needed an institute of social service training, established and maintained by the Government and by the principal universities and voluntary societies, in which courses of varying length will be held for social workers, urban and rural, official and unofficial, according to their education and past experience. Such an institute would be staffed by qualified teachers of economic and social science, and would cover in its courses an analysis of social welfare methods in other countries as well as a study of the needs of India.

44. (4) The provincial schemes are costly, but so in the beginning they must be. In proportion to the results attained they are probably much more costly than Martandam, Khed Shivapur, or similar local centres. But the latter are local, and are supervised by men too rare at present in India for their methods to be reproduced in all parts of the country. A national or a provincial scheme must utilize the average material available within its jurisdiction and must do its best in unpromising as well as in promising villages. The cost of such large-scale work will be diminished when unofficial workers are recruited and voluntary societies are formed ; and will be borne more readily, in the shape of taxes or rates, when the people, especially the younger generation, become accustomed to a higher standard of living and amenities, regard it as normal, and are willing and able (through the prosperity which economic welfare brings) to pay for it.

The District Staff and Rural Development

45. The District Officer, and under him the Assistant Collector or Assistant Commissioner, is now occupied in ways which would have seemed strange to the administrator of fifty years ago. Two outstanding changes have taken place within that period. In the first place, the number of officers of the central Government, the provincial Government, and the local authorities who tour in the villages, visit the towns, and also touch the unspecialized administration of the District Officer by their specialized interests, is much greater than it used to be. In addition to the revenue officers and the police, there are officers of the agricultural, co-operative, education, health, public works (roads or irrigation), and veterinary departments frequently on tour. Less frequently come representatives of many technical or scientific departments, all of whom concern both the District Officer and the private citizen, and whose work can be rendered more beneficial if the District Officer acts as a connecting link between them all.* He may find occasion to suggest collaboration between two or more of them for a common object or between any of them and voluntary associations or private persons having the same interest. The District Officer of to-day devotes less and less of his time to trying legal cases and is hard put to it to supervise even the collection of land revenue, for which he was supposed primarily to exist. Secondly, the Indian public in town and country is alive to its rights and vocal in demanding them. This is a natural and healthy sign of growth, but it means that, if the administration is not to be simply repressive—and under the new system the public can always check repression by electing a new assembly or upsetting the ministry—the administrator must and should busy himself with the promotion of social and economic welfare, whether through local authorities (municipal councils, district boards, union boards, *panchayats*), or voluntary societies, instead of attempting to do the work himself. He is seldom now the chairman of a local authority, but can still serve the common interest as their adviser. He holds more often a post of chairman in a semi-official development board or community council of his district and may be patron or honorary president of any quantity of urban institu-

* Here are some of the occasional but not unimportant departments to which touring officers belong: archaeology, audit, excise, forests, geology, income-tax, industries, meteorology, opium, post office, railways, recruiting, salt, survey, and transport registration. The list is not complete.

tions. In this capacity his usefulness is in direct proportion : (1) to his sympathy and good temper : enthusiasts are often long-winded ; (2) to his judgment : reformers may be hasty or timid ; (3) to his knowledge of the methods employed by local authorities and voluntary societies in other parts of India and in other countries. The Assistant Collector requires just the same qualities as his superior, though his suggestions may be more tentative and he will often refer a question back to the District Officer. Judgment and sympathy are to some extent inborn virtues, but may also be acquired by thought and self-control. Knowledge, on the other hand, is a matter of hard work, and it is open to any servant of government to acquire it and to enhance thereby his value as an adviser. A young Assistant Collector should set himself to learn, without aspiring to become an expert, what every department of government within range of him is doing or trying to do. Personal acquaintance with every kind of "miscellaneous" touring officer affords opportunity for mutual understanding. There has in the past been loss of time and labour through excessive separation and parallelism of departments. In the second place, he should discover what voluntary associations and groups are active in the districts, making the acquaintance, if possible, of their leaders ; though he should not venture to advise them until he has gained knowledge and experience. These associations may at present be weak, but they will be more and more important as Indian life becomes complex and the desire for social welfare general. They are a necessary element in the life of a modern people and no government can now fulfil its task without their assistance. The District Officer is likely to find himself very dependent on them for support in his endeavours to reach and convince the people, and though they may not always be docile, ideally prudent, or continuously energetic, they are far the best agency which he can use. While searching for such unofficial social workers, the Assistant Collector, English or Indian, should not forget the missionaries, English and Indian. They see social conditions from an angle at which he can never stand, some of them enjoy the confidence of the people more than the servants of government, and they are not solely engaged in proselytization. Non-Christian social workers often possess equal knowledge and command equal confidence.

ABOUT THE EDITOR

Pramod K. Nayar teaches at the Department of English, University of Hyderabad. His works on British India include, *English Writing and India, 1600-1920* (2008), *The Great Uprising* (2007), *Colonial Voices* (2012), *The British Raj: Keywords* (2017) and *Indian Travel Writing in the Age of Empire* (Bloomsbury 2020). He has edited *The Trial of Bahadur Shah Zafar* (2007), *The Penguin 1857 Reader* (2007), *Days of the Raj* (2009), *Women in Colonial India* (5 volumes, 2013), *English Siege and Prison Writings* (2016), *Indian Travel Writing, 1830-1947* (5 volumes, 2016) and *Colonial Education in India* (5 volumes, 2019). Besides these, he has also published extensively on Human Rights and Literature, the graphic novel and celebrity culture.